LEGENDS

52 People Who Made a Difference

Bio-Sketches for
Reading, Telling, Listening, Writing, and Research

Graded Readings from American History

Michael Ryall

with illustrations by Len Shalansky

PRO LINGUA ASSOCIATES

Pro Lingua Associates
P. O. Box 1348
Brattleboro, Vermont 05302 USA
Office: 802-257-7779
Orders: 800-366-4775
Email: info@ProLinguaAssociates.com
WebStore: www.ProLinguaAssociates.com
SAN 216-0579

*At **Pro Lingua**,
our objective is to foster
an approach to learning and teaching that
we call **Interplay**, the **inter**action of language
learners and teachers with their materials,
with the language and the culture, and
with each other in active, creative,
and productive **play**.*

ISBN 0-86647-224-X

This book was designed and set in type by Arthur A. Burrows. Adobe *Century Schoolbook* is the type face used for both text and display. It is a digital adaptation of one of the most popular faces of the 20th Century. Century's distinctive roman and italic fonts and its clear, dark strokes and serifs were designed, as the name suggests, to make schoolbooks easy to read. The original, elegant type was cut in 1924 by Morris Fuller Benton for the American Type Foundry of Elizabeth, New Jersey, (the largest and one of the most distinguished type foundries in the United States from 1892 to 1993). It was adapted by Monotype in 1928, and since then many "Century" and "Schoolbook" faces have been developed, as typesetting and printing technology have evolved from Linotype and film to digital design. The book was printed and bound by Boyd Printing Company in Albany, New York.

Printed in the United States of America
First edition, first printing 2006
2,000 copies in print.

Contents

> **A** = Easiest; about 100 words
> **B** = Easy; about 150 words
> **C** = Harder; about 200 words
> **D** = Hardest; about 250 words

Contents

Contents

Business and Labor Leaders   57

Famous Presidents   65

Military Leaders and Heroes   73

Writers   81

Contents

Entertainers   89

Sports Heroes   97

Appendices   105

Introduction

This collection of 52 bio-sketches can be used by English language learners at **high beginning to advanced levels**. It can be used to work on **all skills** — speaking, listening, reading, and writing. At the same time it can be used to explore **American history** through the lives of some very interesting and impressive people.

There are 13 groups of bio-sketches, four people in each group. Within each group of four bio-sketches there are four **different proficiency levels.** The first bio-sketch is the easiest **(Level A), at about 100 words** in length. The second is at **150 (Level B),** the third, **200 (Level C),** and the fourth, **250 (Level D).** In addition to the length of the text, the sentence length and the lexical and grammatical challenge increase along with the word count. Thus the material can be used with classes that have a mixture of proficiency levels, or if the learners are all at the same level, they can first do the 13 easy bio-sketches, then go on to the 13 longer, more challenging texts, and so on through the complete collection.

On the back side of each text there is a **timeline**. On the left side of the timeline are events in the person's life, and on the right side are national events and events from the lives of a few of the other people in this collection. The timeline helps establish the historical context within which the legends lived. Suggestions for using the timelines and CDs are on pages xiii-xiv.

The pages are **perforated**. They can be left intact as a book of 52 readings so that each student will have a complete text. Or, just one or just a few copies of the text can be used with the entire class. In this case, the learners work on selected pages handed out by the teacher. For example, one learner has "Johnny Appleseed," another has "Nat Love," a third one has "Annie Oakley," etc.

These bio-sketches can be used for a variety of purposes.
In addition to being a unique way to explore American history and culture and the Americans who helped make it, learners will be able to sharpen their linguistic skills in a variety of interesting and enjoyable ways. Some suggestions follow.

1. Read and Tell. Each learner is assigned a different legend. They read the text, looking up unfamiliar words or asking for help as the teacher circulates to offer it. When the learner thinks they can tell the story of the legend's life, they find another learner who has a different legend. The two learners then tell each other about their legend. *(Optional: they can do this while looking at the timeline for guidance.)* When they have finished, they can find new partners to tell and listen to. *Note:* the intention here is for the learners to read and understand the text, but then put it in their own words, incorporating words and phrases from the text.

2. *Role Play*. Each learner is given a different legend. They read the text for understanding (dictionaries and the teacher can be consulted). Then two learners pair up . They can simply introduce themselves and tell each other who they are. However, they can also carry on a question-answer conversation, for example: "Why are you a legend?" "When did you do that?" "How old were you when . . .?" "When you did that I was . . ." etc. This can also be done in groups of 3-5 learners.

3. *Read and Write*. The learners read their text (if everyone has a copy of the book, they can all read the same bio-sketch). Then when they are ready, they turn the page over and write the story using the timeline as a guide. Finally, they can compare their stories with a partner or simply compare with the original text.

4. *Interview*. This can be done in a variety of ways. Basically, one learner is the focus of the class, assuming the role of a legend. The teacher or one of the learners assumes the role of host and interviews the guest "legend" while the others listen. It can also be done as a kind of talk show with the listeners "calling in" with questions and comments.

5. *Discussion*. Assign 3-5 different learners different legends who lived at the same time (check the timelines on pages 105 through 108). One learner begins with a statement about their legend. A good opening line is "I was born in 1863. What were you doing at that time?" The learners consult their own timelines, and use their imaginations. "Well, in 1863 I was living in Baltimore, and there was a civil war. How did that affect you?"

6. Dictations. Select one of the legends. *(**Optional:** each student should have a copy of the legend's timeline for guidance.)* Read the text through once deliberately, but not stopping, as the learners follow along. Then read the passage phrase by phrase, allowing a reasonable amount of time for the learners to write each phrase. When the dictation is complete, have the learners compare their writing, and then hand out a copy of the text.

7. Note-Taking. Select a legend and tell one bio-sketch in lecture fashion with reference to the national events listed on the timeline. *(**Optional:** give each learner a copy of the legend's timeline.)* The learners take notes (not complete dictation). Then in pairs or small groups the learners share their notes. They can reconstruct the lecture on a piece of poster paper. Finally, they write a full text based on their collective notes. This activity may work better using one of the longer texts with more advanced learners.

8. Research. After the learners have read and worked with the information about their legend, they can go to the Internet to learn more and write an expanded bio-sketch, or write in greater detail about some aspect or event in the legend's life. A starting point for the research is the web address given at the bottom of the timeline page.

9. Guessing Game Review 1. After the class is familiar with several of the legends, give each one a different legend and an index card. The learners pair up and talk to each other without revealing the name of their legend. After a pair talks to each other for a minute or so (you can ring a bell to signal that it's time to change partners), they split and make a note on their index card: **"Julio >> Thomas Edison?"** After 10 or 15 minutes of meeting, talking, and writing down their guesses, the action stops and the teacher has the class identify each person, one by one:

> *T:* OK, who is Julio?
> *S1:* I think he is Thomas Edison.
> *S2:* I'm not sure. Maybe he is George Washington Carver.
> *S3:* Oh no, he is definitely Edison.
>   etc.
> *T:* So, Julio, who are you?
> *J:* I am the great inventor Thomas Edison.

10. Guessing Game Review 2. After the learners are familiar with several of the legends, tape a copy of the text of one of the legends to the back of each learner, being sure the learner doesn't know who they are. Then they mill around asking questions, trying to identify themselves. You might want to limit each exchange between pairs to two or three questions, just to promote mingling and to have the knowers review the information on more than one legend.

> *Ahmed:* Rosa, when was I born?
> *Rosa:* (Looking at the text taped to Ahmed's back) 1805.
> *Ahmed:* Where was I born?
> *Rosa:* Let's see . . . Kentucky.
> *Amed:* Hmm, OK, thanks. Lee, when did I die?
> *Lee:* You died in 1865.
>   etc.

The timelines give the collection an additional dimension. As noted earlier, the left side of the timeline features events in the legend's life, echoing the information in the passage. The right side of the timeline notes national events and events from the lives of a few other legends. The names in boldface are other legends featured in this collection.

Note that the phrases on the left side are usually incomplete sentences, and the verbs are mostly in the active voice. On the right side the phrases can stand alone as sentences, and they are often in the passive voice. This allows the students to construct statements such as these (the phrase in bold is explicit on the time line):

Thomas Edison **moved to New York City** in 1869. (from the left side)

In 1871, **Chicago was destroyed by a great fire**. (from the right side)

Edison **started a research lab** in 1876, and also in 1876 **the telephone was developed by Alexander Graham Bell.**

In 1879, Edison **invented the electric light bulb.**

In America, (in 1898) **the Spanish-American War began** (in 1898).

Throughout the right-side timelines, there are references to U.S. Presidents. To help place these references in the larger context of U.S. history, a list of the Presidents is included on page 109.

Introduction

The timelines can be used in a variety of ways:

1. Learners use the left side only as a series of prompts as they retell the legend's life.

2. The learners can use both sides to retell a fuller account of the life and times of the legend. For example, if the learner is working on Edison, they will encounter (on the right side of the timeline), "inventor **George Washington Carver** was born." The boldface indicates that Carver is one of the legends in the collection. This could lead the learners to read about and study Carver's life next.

3. Many of the notations may not mean much to the learners. Making the phrase meaningful can be the next step. For example, the learners read "the Spanish-American War began." The next step could be to have the learners go to the library or encyclopedia or Internet to find out about the Spanish-American War and then report on it or discuss it in the next class.

4. As an alternative to the above suggestion, individuals or pairs can research different national events mentioned in the right-side timeline. For example (from the timeline for Edison):

> *Julio and Jorge, find out about Samuel Morse.*
> *Maria and Lupita, research the Great Chicago Fire.*
> *Luis and Felipe, find more information about Alexander
> Graham Bell.*

Using the legends and the timelines can bring American history to life.

Introduction

**The 52 bio-sketches in this collection are available
as 52 separate tracks on a CD** *(see the table of contents for a listing).*

The recordings can be used in a variety of ways. Some suggestions follow:

1. The collection can be used primarily for listening comprehension practice. If everyone is working on the same passage, play the CD track. Then have the students read the passage, and finally have them look at the timeline and play the passage again. Obviously, after the listening, the class can write the passage from memory, and then compare it with the original. They can discuss the passage and the timeline. They can also create a few comprehension questions and quiz each other. And in pairs they can reconstruct the passage orally, taking turns saying something about the legend.

2. Play the recording and have the students read along with the recording. This can be done just for the listening-reading practice, or it can be a preparation step before having the students reconstruct the passage orally from memory or by using the timeline prompts.

3. Play the recording and by using the pause button, have the students take dictation. After the dictation, they can refer to the original passage to check the accuracy of their writing.

4. If a listening lab is available, the students can use the text and the recording for self-study purposes.

•   •   •   •

Obviously, there are many more ways this collection can be used. E-mail us (Info@ProLinguaAssociates.com) a description of your idea and we'll put it on our web site.

Johnny Appleseed

1774–1845

Johnny Appleseed's real name was John Chapman. He was born in Massachusetts on September 26,1774. There are lots of stories about Johnny Appleseed. Some are true and some aren't. In the early 1800s, Johnny arrived in the Ohio River Valley. He began to grow apple trees from seeds. He sold trees, and he gave many trees away. Johnny died in Fort Wayne, Indiana, in 1845. Other people took his seeds all the way across the country to California. Today there are apple trees everywhere in America.

TIMELINE

Johnny Appleseed		America
John Chapman was born in Massachusetts	**1774**	
	1775	the American Revolution began at the Battle of Lexington and Concord
	1789	**George Washington** became President
arrived in the Ohio River Valley grew apple trees traveled in the Midwest	**early 1800s**	
	1801	Thomas Jefferson became President
	1804-1806	**Sacagawea,** Lewis, and Clark explored the Louisiana Purchase
	1809	**Abraham Lincoln** was born in Kentucky
	1812	war began between the United States and Great Britain
	1820	**Daniel Boone** died
	1825	the Erie Canal was opened
	1840	**Chief Joseph** was born
died on March 10	**1845**	

Research:
www.millville.org/Workshops_f/Dich_FOLKLORE/WACKED/story.html

Nat Love

1854–1921

Nat Love was born a slave in 1854. He got his freedom when he was 11 years old. In his teens, Nat lived in Dodge City, Kansas. He was in a group of cowboys called the Duval Outfit. Nat entered a roping contest at the age of 22. He roped a cow in nine minutes. People called him the "Champion Roper of the Western Cattle Country."

Steam trains came to the West in the late 1800s. Many cowboys got jobs on the railroad. Nat took a job as a porter. Sometimes he missed riding horses and roping cows. But he had lots of stories to tell the passengers. Soon he became very popular.

In 1907 Nat wrote the story of his life. It was called *The Life and Adventures of Nat Love.* Nat told about the places he had been and the things he had done. He died in 1921.

TIMELINE

Nat Love		America
was born a slave	**1854**	
	1860	**President Lincoln** was elected the South prepared to fight
	1863	**Lincoln** issued the Emancipation Proclamation
got his freedom	**1865**	the Civil War ended
	1868	former slaves got citizenship
	1869	the Transcontinental Railroad was completed
became a cowboy entered a roping contest	**1876**	the Battle of the Little Bighorn was fought
	1885	**Annie Oakley** joined Buffalo Bill's show
left the cowboy life took a job as a Pullman porter	**1890**	
	1901	oil was discovered in Texas
wrote the story of his life	**1907**	
died	**1921**	

Research:

www.natlove.com/

Daniel Boone

1734–1820

Nobody is quite sure when Daniel Boone was born. Most people think that he was born around 1734. As a young man, Daniel was a hunter and trapper. He knew how to live in the wilderness. In 1775 he got a job making trails. He made a trail called the Wilderness Road. He started a settlement on the Wilderness Road. The settlement was called Boonesboro.

The settlers in Boonesboro went to war with the Shawnee, a Native American tribe. In 1778 the Shawnee kidnapped Daniel. He lived with the Shawnee for five months. Then he escaped and ran back to Boonesboro. He warned the settlers that the Shawnee were coming. Daniel saved the settlers.

Ten years later, Daniel decided to leave Boonesboro. He said it was "too crowded." He traveled in a canoe to Missouri. He lived there for the rest of his life.

Daniel died at the age of 86. At first, he was buried in Missouri. Twenty-five years later, his body was moved to Boonesboro. His grave is in a cemetery on top of a hill.

TIMELINE

Daniel Boone		America
was born in a cabin in the woods	**1734**	
	1754	the French and Indian War began
built a trail called the Wilderness Road started the town of Boonesboro	**1775**	The Revolutionary War began **Washington** was named commander in chief **John Paul Jones** was chosen commander of the navy
was kidnapped by Shawnee Indians escaped and saved the town of Boonesboro	**1778**	France joined the war on the American side
	1781	the British army surrendered at Yorktown, ending the war
moved to Missouri	**1788**	
	1789	**Washington** became President
	1803	the U.S. bought the Louisiana Territory
	1804	**Sacagawea,** Lewis, and Clark began exploring the West
	1812	war with Britain started
died September 26	**1820**	the Missouri Compromise limited the spread of slavery to new states
Daniel's body was moved to Boonesboro	**1845**	

Research:
www.lucidcafe.com/library/95nov/boone.html

Annie Oakley

1860–1926

Annie Oakley was born in 1860 in Ohio. Her full name was Phoebe Ann Oakley Moses. Her mother called her Phoebe, but her sisters called her Annie. The family was poor. Annie's father had died shortly after she was born. To help her mother, Annie learned how to hunt with a rifle. At the age of nine, she could hit anything with her rifle.

As a young woman, Annie entered a shooting contest with a man named Frank Butler. Annie won the contest, and she fell in love with Frank. They got married and went into show business. Frank and Annie went to vaudeville shows and circuses. People paid money to watch them shoot targets. Annie was a perfect shooter. Her fame spread far and wide.

In 1885 Annie joined Buffalo Bill's Wild West Show. It had cowboys, Native Americans, and sharpshooters. Sitting Bull, a Native American leader, was in the show. He called Annie "Little Miss Sure Shot." He gave her that name because she was only five feet tall. Annie was in Buffalo Bill's show for 17 years.

Annie's tricks were amazing. She could shoot a card five times before it hit the ground. She could aim by looking in a mirror. Annie kept her perfect aim, even in old age. She died in 1926, at the age of sixty-six. Her husband Frank died that same year.

TIMELINE

Annie Oakley		America
was born August 18 in Ohio	**1860**	**President Lincoln** was elected the Civil War began
	1865	the Civil War ended
became an expert shot with a rifle	**1869**	U.S. Grant became President
beat Frank Butler in a shooting contest	**1876**	**Nat Love** became a cowboy
joined Buffalo Bill's show	**1881**	**Clara Barton** began theAmerican Red Cross
	1885	
left Buffalo Bill's show	**1902**	
	1908	Henry Ford mass produced the Model T car
raised money for the Red Cross on a national shooting tour	**1917**	the U.S. entered World War I
	1920	**Amelia Earhart** learned to fly
	1924	the U.S. Congress passed a law making all Indians citizens
died	**1926**	

Research:

www.cowgirls.com/dream/cowgals/oakley.htm

Harriet Tubman

1821 –1913

Harriet Tubman was born in Maryland in 1821. All the members of her family were slaves. The woman in charge of Harriet whipped her every day. Harriet decided to run away. She escaped, and she reached the free state of Pennsylvania. It was her first taste of freedom. She wanted to share her freedom with others.

Harriet went back to Maryland secretly for her sister. They walked through the woods at night. They followed the North Star. Slave hunters chased them. The trip was dangerous, but Harriet went back for her brother. Six years later, she freed her parents. Harriet made 19 trips, and rescued more than 300 slaves.

TIMELINE

Harriet Tubman		America
was born in Maryland	**1821**	
	1828	Andrew Jackson was elected President
	1838	the "Trail of Tears" killed many Cherokee people
escaped to freedom	**1849**	
helped sister escape	**1850**	the Fugitive Slave Law was strengthened
helped brother escape	**1851**	
	1852	*Uncle Tom's Cabin* was published
rescued parents	**1857**	
	1861	the Southern states seceded
	1863	**Lincoln** issued the Emancipation Proclamation
	1865	**General Robert E. Lee** surrendered to U.S. Grant. **Lincoln** was shot
	1876	Alexander Graham Bell invented the telephone
died	**1913**	

Research:

www.civilwarhome.com/tubmanbio.htm

Clara Barton

1821–1912

Clara Barton was born in Massachusetts in 1821. As a young woman, she was a schoolteacher. But in 1861 the Civil War began. It was a bloody and deadly war. Nurses and doctors were needed on the battlefield. Clara decided to become a nurse.

In addition to her duties as a nurse, she distributed supplies for wounded soldiers. She also set up a system to search for missing men. Clara became known as the "Angel of the Battlefield."

The Civil War ended in 1865, but Clara continued her work as a nurse. In 1881 she founded the American Red Cross, and she was its president until 1904. Clara died in 1912, but the American Red Cross exists today. It helps people who are affected by wars and natural disasters. That was Clara's dream, and her dream came true.

TIMELINE

Clara Barton		America
was born in Massachusetts	**1821**	Troy Female Seminary was opened
	1824	John Quincy Adams was elected President
	1826	**Sojourner Truth** escaped from slavery
became a schoolteacher at the age of 15	**1836**	the fall of the Alamo; Texans take Texas from Mexico
	1846	in Mexican-American War, the U.S. gained Texas and California
	1848	gold was discovered in California
became a nurse in the Civil War	**1861**	the Civil War began
	1865	**General Lee** surrendered
began the American Red Cross	**1881**	
	1898	the Spanish-American War began
resigned as president of the Red Cross	**1904**	
	1906	an earthquake destroyed San Francisco
died on April 12	**1912**	Woodrow Wilson was elected President

Research:

www.civilwarhome.com/bartonbio.htm

Frederick Douglass

1817–1895

Frederick Douglass was born in Maryland. He was the son of a slave. He was taken away from his mother to a plantation at the age of six. Frederick was treated very badly. He had to eat out of a trough, and he slept on the floor. He had only one shirt and no sheets or blankets.

When Frederick was about ten he was taken to Baltimore. He decided to learn how to read and write. He asked poor white children to be his teachers, and he paid them with pieces of bread. His master screamed at him whenever he caught Frederick reading. It was against the law for slaves to read or write. One day Frederick's master whipped Frederick. Frederick decided to fight back. He and his master fought for two hours. In Frederick's mind, he stopped being a slave on that day.

In 1838 Frederick fled to New York, running from slave catchers along the way. In New York and Boston, Frederick gave speeches and wrote against slavery. He started an anti-slavery newspaper called the North Star. Frederick lived to see the end of slavery. In 1889 he became the U.S. minister to Haiti. His autobiography is now considered to be a classic.

TIMELINE

Frederick Douglass		America
was born in Maryland	**1817**	James Monroe became President
moved to Baltimore	**1826**	the Erie Canal was opened
escaped to New York	**1838**	
wrote his autobiography	**1845**	
started the *North Star*	**1847**	
	1852	*Uncle Tom's Cabin* was published
	1857	The Supreme Court makes the Dred Scott decision on slavery
	1860	**Annie Oakley** was born
	1861	the South seceded from Union
	1883	**Sojourner Truth** died
	1884	*Huckleberry Finn* was published
became Minister to Haiti	**1889**	
	1890	the Battle of Wounded Knee was fought
died at the age of 78	**1895**	

Research:

www.pbs.org/wgbh/aia/part4/4p1539.html

Sojourner Truth

1797–1883

Sojourner Truth was born in New York State in 1797. Her given name was Isabella. Her parents were both slaves, and so was she. She knew only one of her 11 brothers and sisters. The others were sold to different slave owners before she was born.

By the time she was 20, Isabella had also been sold several times to different masters. As a slave, she had to do all kinds of work: cooking, cleaning, working in the fields. During this time, she had two children. The slave owner sold them both. Once again, Isabella was separated from her family. She decided to escape, first to a neighbor's house and then to New York City.

At a religious festival, Isabella had a powerful religious experience. She heard voices and saw visions. She wanted to share her experience, so she started to sing, pray, and preach. Isabella changed her name to Sojourner, which means "traveler," and she traveled from town to town in the Northeast and Midwest.

Wherever Sojourner went, she spoke out against slavery and for women's rights. In 1865 slavery finally came to an end. Sojourner helped freed slaves to find work and a place to live. She encouraged thousands of African Americans to settle in Kansas. Many of their descendants still live there to this day.

Sojourner worked for equal rights until she was too old to travel. Then she settled down in her home in Battle Creek, Michigan. That is where she died on November 26, 1883.

TIMELINE

Sojourner Truth		America
was born in New York State	**1797**	John Adams became President
	1821	**Clara Barton** was born
escaped from slavery	**1826**	**Frederick Douglass** moved to Baltimore, Maryland
had a powerful religious experience	**1827**	
moved to New York City	**1829**	
	1833	Oberlin College accepted female students
	1838	the Cherokee Indians were forced to move to Oklahoma
became a traveling preacher	**1843**	
helped freed slaves find work and a place to live	**1865**	the Civil War ended
	1872	**Susan B. Anthony** was arrested for trying to vote
died in her home in Battle Creek, Michigan	**1883**	the Brooklyn Bridge was completed

Research:

www.lkwdpl.org/wihohio/trut-soj.htm

Chief Joseph

1840–1904

Chief Joseph was a Native American leader. In the late 1800s, the U.S. government forced many Native Americans to live on reservations. Then the government began to take away some of the reservations. Chief Joseph fought for his people's land. He wanted to avoid war, but he and his people, the Nez Perce, had to fight back. They won many battles, but the U.S. Army used guns. After three months, Chief Joseph had to surrender. The U.S. government forced Chief Joseph and his people to leave their land. Chief Joseph said, "I am tired of fighting . . . I will fight no more forever."

TIMELINE

Chief Joseph		America
was born in Oregon	**1840**	
	1844	**Sarah Winnemucca** was born
	1846	the Mexican War was fought
	1865	**Lincoln** was assassinated
	1869	the Transcontinental Railroad was completed
became chief of the Nez Perce	**1871**	
refused to give land to the U.S. government	**1876**	General Custer was defeated at the Battle of the Little Bighorn
went to war with the U.S. Army in June surrendered in October	**1877**	
	1883	the Northern Pacific Railroad was finished
	1886	the Statue of Liberty was opened
	1890	many Indians were massacred at the Battle of Wounded Knee
	1895	**Frederick Douglass** died
died on a reservation in Washington state	**1904**	

Research:

www.pbs.org/weta/thewest/people/a_c/chiefjoseph.htm

Sitting Bull

1834–1890

Sitting Bull was probably born in 1834. In his youth, other children called him "Slow." When he was ten, Slow killed his first buffalo. He gave the meat to a poor family that needed food. Later, at the age of 14, Slow fought bravely in a battle. His courage and generosity earned him the name "Sitting Bull." To be named after a bull was a great honor. It was the name of a leader.

In 1869 Sitting Bull became Chief of the Sioux nation. Five years later, the U.S. government sent General Custer to fight the Sioux for their land. Custer led his army in an attack against the Sioux at a place called the Little Bighorn. Sitting Bull and other Sioux leaders destroyed Custer's army. In 1881 Sitting Bull surrendered. He traveled with Buffalo Bill's Wild West Show for a while. In 1890 while he was being arrested, he was killed.

TIMELINE

Sitting Bull		America
"Slow" was born	**1834**	
	1840	**Chief Joseph** was born
	1841	wagon trains began moving west with settlers
was named "Sitting Bull"	**1848**	gold was discovered in California
became chief of the Sioux	**1869**	Grant became President. the Transcontinental Railroad was finished in Utah
the U.S. government decided to take land from the Sioux	**1874**	
General Custer's army was destroyed at the Little Bighorn in Montana	**1876**	the telephone was invented
Sitting Bull surrendered	**1881**	
became a friend of Buffalo Bill	**1885**	**Annie Oakley** and **Sitting Bull** joined Buffalo Bill's Wild West Show
killed during arrest	**1890**	many Indians were massacred at Wounded Knee

Research:

www.pbs.org/weta/thewest/people/s_z/sittingbull.htm

Sequoyah

1770–1842

Sequoyah was born about 1770 in the Smoky Mountains of Tennessee. He was a Cherokee Indian. When he was small, his mother told him many traditional stories. Sequoyah loved to listen to them.

In the 1700s, the Cherokee did not have a writing system. They told their stories from memory. As time passed, people showed less interest in storytelling. The stories were slowly disappearing. Sequoyah wanted to save this important tradition. He decided to create a writing system for the Cherokee language.

Sequoyah started his work in 1814. He created a written symbol for every syllable in the Cherokee language. Finally, in 1821, Sequoyah was finished. He had created a total of 86 symbols. Some of the symbols looked like letters from the English alphabet. Other symbols were completely new. Sequoyah taught other members of his tribe how to read his symbols. In 1828 he started a newspaper called the *Cherokee Phoenix.* It was the first Native American newspaper in history.

In 1838 the U.S. government forced the Cherokee to move to Oklahoma. Sequoyah died there five years later. At the time, he was trying to create a writing system for another Native American language.

TIMELINE

Sequoyah		America
was born in the Smoky Mountains	**1770**	
	1775	the American Revolution began
	1799	**George Washington** died
started working on the Cherokee writing system	**1814**	the British burned the U.S. Capitol and the White House Andrew Jackson defeated the Creek Indians at Horseshoe Bend
	1820	**Daniel Boone** died the Missouri Compromise was passed
completed the writing system	**1821**	
started a newspaper called the *Cherokee Phoenix*	**1828**	Jackson was elected President the Baltimore & Ohio, first passenger railroad in the U.S., began
	1836	the battles of the Alamo and San Jacinto were fought in Texas
	1837	Martin Van Buren, Jackson's Vice President, became President
was forced to move to Oklahoma by the U.S. government (The Trail of Tears)	**1838**	the Indian Territory of Oklahoma was established
died while trying to create a writing system for another Native American language	**1842**	the Seminole War ended many Seminoles were moved from Florida to Oklahoma

Research:

www.powersource.com/gallery/people/sequoyah.html

Annie Dodge Wauneka

1910–1997

Annie understood that traditional ways of healing were also important. She worked with Native Indian medicine men. They used herbs and ceremonies to heal the sick. Annie wanted to combine traditional forms of healing with modern medicine. Gradually, people accepted her ideas. Medicine men actually began to work with doctors!

Health standards began to improve. The life span of Navajos also increased. For her efforts, Annie received the Presidential Medal of Freedom in 1963. She was the first Native American to receive this award. And in 2000 Annie was admitted into the National Women's Hall of Fame.

Annie Dodge Wauneka was born on a Navajo reservation in 1910. When she was just eight years old there was a flu epidemic at the reservation. Annie survived, but thousands of other children on the reservation died. This tragedy shaped the rest of Annie's life.

Annie's father was chief of the Navajo. Annie learned about leadership from him. In 1951 she was elected to the Navajo Tribal Council. Her goal as a tribal leader was to improve health conditions on the reservation. Annie never wanted another tragedy like the one she experienced.

In 1960 Annie started giving talks on the radio. She explained the importance of modern medicine. Many Navajos did not trust doctors and hospitals. Annie had to overcome their fear of "white medicine."

221 words

TIMELINE

Annie Dodge Wauneka		America
	1908	Henry Ford created the Model T
was born on a Navajo reservation	**1910**	**Jacqueline Cochran** was born
survived the great flu epidemic	**1918**	U.S. joined World War I in Europe
	1920	the 19th Amendment gave women the right to vote
	1945	Navajo code talkers helped defeat the Japanese; World War II ended
was elected to the Navajo Tribal Council	**1951**	
started giving weekly health talks on the radio	**1960**	**John Kennedy** was elected President
was awarded the Presidential Medal of Freedom	**1963**	Kennedy was assassinated. Lyndon Johnson became President
	1968	**Martin Luther King, Jr.** was assassinated
	1993	**Cesar Chavez** died
died at the age of 87	**1997**	
was admitted to the National Women's Hall of Fame	**2000**	Scientists completed mapping the human genome

Research:

www.greatwomen.org/women.php?action=viewone&id=166

Thomas Alva Edison

1847–1931

Thomas Edison was born in Ohio. As a young boy, he loved to read and learn. He was taught at home by his mother. He became very interested in electricity. In 1869 he decided to become a scientist and moved to New York City. In 1876 he started a research laboratory in Newark, New Jersey. He called it Menlo Park.

The next year, Edison invented the phonograph. Two years later, he invented the electric light bulb. Later, he experimented with motion pictures. He made "The Great Train Robbery," the first movie that told a story. He never stopped working. In total, he created more than 1,100 inventions.

TIMELINE

Thomas Alva Edison		**_America_**
	1844	Samuel Morse invented the telegraph
was born in Ohio	**1847**	
	1861	inventor **George Washington Carver** was born
moved to New York City	**1869**	
	1871	Chicago was destroyed in a great fire
started a research laboratory in Newark, New Jersey	**1876**	the telephone was developed by Alexander Graham Bell
invented the phonograph player	**1877**	
invented the electric light bulb	**1879**	
	1898	the Spanish-American War began
	1902	**Andrew Carnegie** started the Carnegie Institute
produced the first movie to tell a story	**1903**	Henry Ford founded the Ford Motor Company
	1917	the U.S. entered World War I
died at the age of 84	**1931**	the Empire State Building was built

Research:

www.lucidcafe.com/library/96feb/edison.html

Dian Fossey

1932–1985

Dian Fossey was interested in animals all her life. She was especially interested in wild animals. In 1963 she went to East Africa to see mountain gorillas for herself. Dian immediately fell in love with these beautiful animals.

In 1967 Dian moved to Rwanda to study the gorillas in their natural habitat. She learned that gorillas were being shot and killed by hunters. She became very concerned. The gorillas were in danger of extinction.

One day, Dian's favorite gorilla Digit was killed. So Dian decided to do something. In 1983 she wrote a book called *Gorillas in the Mist.* She wanted the world to know that the gorillas were in danger. Five years later, the book became a film. People around the world asked the government of Rwanda to do something. Today, the gorillas are protected, thanks in part to Dian Fossey. Sadly, Dian was murdered in 1985.

TIMELINE

Dian Fossey		America
was born in San Francisco, California	**1932**	
	1941	America entered World War II
	1960	**Zora Neale Hurston** died Jane Goodall began studying chimpanzees in Tanzania
went to East Africa	**1963**	**John Kennedy** was assassinated
moved to Rwanda to study gorillas	**1967**	Dr. Goodall became director of the Gombe Game Reserve
	1968	Robert Kennedy was shot and killed
	1969	the Apollo crew walked on the Moon
went to Cambridge for a PhD	**1970**	the first "Earth Day" was celebrated in the U.S.
poachers killed Digit and his family; Dian declared war on them	**1978**	
wrote *Gorillas in the Mist*	**1983**	
killed at the age of 53	**1985**	the "Live Aid" rock concert was held
Gorillas in the Mist became a film	**1987**	
	1994	the Rwanda civil war/genocide began

Research:
www.unmuseum.org/fossey.htm

Rachel Carson

1907–1964

Rachel Carson was born in a small town on the Allegheny River in Pennsylvania. As a young child, Rachel was interested in animals and nature. She also loved to write, and she decided to be a writer when she grew up.

In college, Rachel combined her love of nature and her passion for writing. She studied both biology and English, graduating with high honors in 1929. After that, Rachel started working for the U.S. Fish and Wildlife Service. She wrote radio plays to educate people about nature.

In 1941 Rachel published her first book. It was called *Under the Sea Wind,* and it was about animals living in the Arctic zone. Rachel published her next book, *The Sea Around Us*, in 1950. It quickly became a best-seller. But Rachel's most famous book was *Silent Spring*, which was published in 1962. In *Silent Spring* she told about the dangers of pesticides and other chemicals. It showed how pesticides traveled through the food chain — from plants to animals and, eventually, human beings.

Soon after that, many laws were passed by the government to control the use of pesticides. With *Silent Spring*, Rachel Carson had started the environmental movement.

196 words

TIMELINE

Rachel Carson		America
	1901	Theodore Roosevelt became President
was born in Pennsylvania	**1907**	
studied biology and English graduated with high honors	**1929**	the stock market crash started the Great Depression
	1937	**Amelia Earhart** disappeared
wrote her first book, *Under the Sea Wind*	**1941**	Pearl Harbor was bombed; the U.S. entered World War II
wrote *The Sea Around Us*	**1950**	
	1955	**Matthew Henson** died
	1959	Alaska and Hawaii became states
wrote her most famous book, *Silent Spring*	**1962**	
died at the age of 57	**1964**	
	1969	the first Environment Protection Act
	1989	the EXXON Valdez oil spill caused an environmental disaster in Alaska

Research:
www.rachelcarson.org

George Washington Carver

1861–1943

George Washington Carver was born into slavery during the Civil War. Like many other slaves, he took the last name of his owner, Moses Carver. Mr. Carver was kind to George, and treated him like a member of his own family.

As a child, George was very curious and intelligent. He dreamed of going to school. At the time, however, African Americans weren't allowed to attend the local school. Mr. Carver helped him get into a different school in another town eight miles away.

George was a good student, but he didn't start college until 1891, when he was about 30 years old. After graduation, George started teaching science classes. He was the first black professor at Iowa State College, and he quickly gained a reputation as an outstanding scientist.

In 1896 George was invited to teach at the Tuskegee Institute, an all-black college in Alabama. George accepted, because he had always wanted to help other African Americans get an education.

In the South, cotton was an important crop. Some farmers planted only cotton. George discovered that it was important to change crops. He told farmers to alternate sweet potatoes and peanuts with cotton. By doing that, the soil kept its nutrients. In his laboratory, George also found other uses for peanuts. He developed over 300 products from the peanut plant. By the time he died, in 1943, he was recognized as the world's greatest plant scientist.

TIMELINE

George W. Carver		America
was born into slavery	**1861**	
	1865	the Civil War ended
	1881	**Booker T. Washington** established Tuskegee Institute
began college at the age of 30	**1891**	
	1892	Ellis Island was opened
started teaching at the Tuskegee Institute	**1896**	
encouraged farmers to start planting soybeans and peanuts	**1890s**	
developed over 300 products from the peanut plant	**1900s**	
	1907	**Rachel Carson** was born
patented soy-based paints	**1927**	
	1931	the Dust Bowl began; the drought continued until 1939
	1932	**Franklin Roosevelt** was elected President
died at the age of 82	**1943**	

Research:

www.lib.iastate.edu/spcl/gwc/home.html

Father Flanagan

1886–1948

Edward Joseph Flanagan was born in Ireland in 1886. He studied in Ireland, Rome, and Austria. In 1912 he became a priest. (People call priests "Father.")

Father Flanagan came to the U. S. in 1914, and settled in Nebraska. There he created a shelter for homeless men. Then in 1917, Father Flanagan started a shelter for homeless boys. Father Flanagan taught these boys the importance of good behavior. They helped run the farm. In 1926 they changed the name of the farm to "Boys Town."

Father Flanagan died in 1948, but his work has continued. In 1978 girls were admitted to Boys Town. Other shelters for homeless children and teens have started all over the country.

TIMELINE

Father Flanagan		America
	1882	**Jane Addams** opened Hull House
was born in Ireland	**1886**	
	1892	Ellis Island was opened
became a Catholic priest	**1912**	
moved to the United States started a shelter for homeless men	**1914**	
started a home for homeless boys in Omaha, Nebraska	**1917**	
	1918	**Annie Dodge Wauneka** survived the great flu epidemic
the shelter's name was changed to Boys Town	**1926**	
	1927	**Cesar Chavez** born
	1930s	the Great Economic Depression
	1938	the movie *Boys Town* starred Spencer Tracy; got two Oscars: best story, best actor
Father Flanagan died	**1948**	
girls admitted to Boys Town	**1978**	

Research:

www.nebraskastudies.org/0700/stories/0702_0101.html

Jane Addams

1860–1935

Jane Addams was born in Illinois in 1860. Her father was a senator, and Jane lived in a very nice house. But she cared about people who were less fortunate. In nearby Chicago, Jane saw many people living in poverty. She decided to do something about it. In 1882 she created a settlement. It was a shelter for the poor, especially for poor women. Jane called it Hull House.

Many immigrants came to Hull House, and they brought their children. Jane taught the children English, music, and art. Their parents took classes in job training. More and more people came. Jane decided to start other settlements like Hull House.

In 1911 Jane started the National Federation of Settlements. The federation organized settlements all over the country. Jane had started an important social movement. She was famous, but she stayed at Hull House all her life. In 1931 she won the Nobel Peace Prize.

TIMELINE

Jane Addams		America
was born in Illinois	**1860**	**Annie Oakley** was born
	1871	Chicago began to be rebuilt after the Great Chicago Fire
	1878	**Edison** invented the electric light
started Hull House, a settlement in Chicago	**1882**	
	1906	an earthquake destroyed San Francisco **Susan B. Anthony** died
started the National Federation of Settlements	**1911**	
	1917	**Father Flanagan** opened his shelter for boys
	1925	**A. Philip Randolph** founded a union for railroad workers
	1929	the Great Depression began; **Martin Luther King, Jr.** was born
won the Nobel Peace Prize for her work for pacifism, women's suffrage, and civil rights	**1931**	**Thomas Edison** died
	1932	**FDR** was elected President: he began the New Deal
died in Chicago	**1935**	

Research:

www.uic.edu/jaddams/hull/ja_bio.html

Booker T. Washington

1856–1915

Booker T. Washington was born into slavery in 1856. Seven years later, all slaves were freed. Booker decided to go to school, but he also had to work. He got a job in a salt mine, digging salt underground. He worked from 4 a.m. until 9 a.m., and then he went to school until 3 p.m. After school, he went back to work for two more hours.

In 1872 Booker went to the Hampton Institute, a school for African Americans. He graduated three years later, and became a teacher.

Booker bought an old farm in 1881. He turned the buildings into classrooms. The school was called the Tuskegee Institute, and it offered courses to African Americans. Booker believed that education should be combined with job training. To help his students get jobs and start their own businesses, he created the National Negro Business League in 1901. A year later, he wrote a book explaining his ideas. It was called *Up From Slavery.*

Booker died at his home in Tuskegee, Alabama, in 1915. The Tuskegee Institute still offers courses in arts and sciences, agriculture, business, and education.

TIMELINE

Booker T. Washington		America
was born into slavery	**1856**	
	1861	the South seceded from the Union
was freed and went to school	**1863**	**Lincoln** delivered the Emancipation Proclamation
attended Hampton Institute	**1872**	
became a teacher	**1875**	
bought a farm and turned it into the Tuskegee Institute	**1881**	**Clara Barton** began the Red Cross
	1884	*Huckleberry Finn* was published
	1886	the Statue of Liberty was opened
	1889	**Frederick Douglass** went to Haiti
created the National Negro Business League	**1901**	oil was discovered in Texas
wrote *Up from Slavery*	**1902**	**Andrew Carnegie** started the Carnegie Foundation
	1910	**Mark Twain** died **Annie Dodge Wauneka** was born
died in Tuskegee, Alabama	**1915**	

Research:
en.wikipedia.org/wiki/Booker_T_Washington

Nellie Bly
1864 –1922

Elizabeth Cochran was born on May 5, 1864, in Pennsylvania. Her father was a judge. When he died the family had to sell their comfortable home. Elizabeth helped raise her siblings. Then her mother remarried, and her stepfather was abusive to the children. Perhaps that led to Elizabeth's work for women's rights.

At the age of 18, Elizabeth wrote a letter to the editor of the *Pittsburgh Dispatch* in response to a sexist editorial. She was hired by the paper as a journalist and changed her name to "Nellie Bly." Her first article, in 1885, was called "The Girl Puzzle." It was about prejudice against women in the workplace.

Nellie is often considered the inventor of investigative reporting. She wrote about sweatshop workers. She wrote about poverty and corruption in Mexico. After returning from Mexico she got a job with the *New York World.* In 1887 she pretended to be a mental patient. She checked into a mental hospital and then wrote an article called "Ten Days in a Mad-House."

In 1889 she became famous when the *New York World* sent her to write about a journey around the world. She challenged the novel *Around the World in Eighty Days*, and completed her trip in just over 72 days. She got a huge welcome when she returned.

In 1914 she was in Europe when World War I began, and she stayed to report on the war from the front lines. Back in New York, Nellie continued to write about the poor, the sick, and the underprivileged until her death in 1922.

TIMELINE

Nellie Bly		America
was born as Elizabeth Cochran	**1864**	
	1867	the U.S. bought Alaska from Russia
	1872	*Around the World in 80 Days* was published in French
wrote to *Pittsburgh Dispatch* protesting a sexist editorial	**1882**	
became a journalist and changed her name to Nellie Bly	**1885**	Grover Cleveland became President
wrote *Ten Days in a Mad-House*	**1887**	
went around the world in 72 days	**1889**	
	1893	Grover Cleveland became President again
	1897	**Amelia Earhart** was born
	1910	**Jaqueline Cochran** was born
reported on World War I	**1914**	the Panama Canal was opened
	1916	Jeanette Rankin became the first female representative in the U.S. Congress
died of pneumonia	**1922**	

Research:

www.nelliebly.org

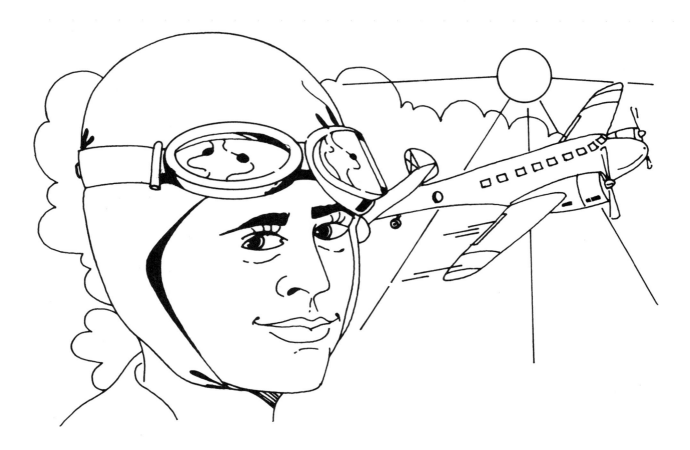

Amelia Earhart

1897–1937

Amelia Earhart was an airplane pilot. She started flying airplanes in 1920. In 1932 Amelia flew across the Atlantic Ocean by herself. Her next goal was to fly around the world.

Amelia and her co-pilot took off on May 20, 1937. They stopped along the way to get more fuel. On July 2, Amelia sent a radio message. She said the fuel was leaking. That was her last message. Amelia and her co-pilot disappeared. Most people think they crashed into the Pacific Ocean. Still today some people try to find Amelia, her co-pilot, and her Electra airplane in the Pacific Ocean.

TIMELINE

Amelia Earhart		America
was born in Atchison, Kansas	**1897**	William McKinley became President
	1898	Guam and Hawaii were annexed by the U.S.
	1903	the Wright brothers first flew a heavier-than-air plane
	1914	fighting airplanes were first used in WWI
	1918	the first regular U.S. airmail service was begun
started flying airplanes	**1920**	the 19th Amendment gave women the right to vote
	1927	Charles Lindbergh flew across the Atlantic alone
was the first woman to fly across the Atlantic by herself	**1932**	**Jacqueline Cochran** got her pilot's license
	1933	**Franklin Roosevelt** became President
began a flight around the world (May 20) disappeared over the Pacific Ocean (July 2)	**1937**	

Research:

www.ameliaearhart.com

Alan Shepard

1923–1998

Alan Shepard was born in 1923. He became a pilot for the U.S. Navy when he was 22. In 1959 he was chosen to be an astronaut. Two years later, he took a test flight in a rocket. The rocket took off from Cape Canaveral, in Florida. It went 117 miles into space, and then returned to Earth. The flight lasted only 15 minutes. Alan had become the first American to fly in space.

Alan's most exciting adventure came in 1971. He was an astronaut on Apollo 14. The goal of Apollo was to explore the moon. Alan was the fifth American to walk on the moon's surface. He collected rock samples and brought them back to Earth.

In 1974 Alan resigned from the astronaut program and the Navy. He died in 1998. Before he died, Alan said: "I must admit, maybe I am a piece of history after all."

TIMELINE

Alan Shepard		America
was born in East Derry, New Hapshire	**1923**	
	1937	**Amelia Earhart** disappeared
	1939	World War II began
became a pilot for the U.S. Navy	**1945**	Harry Truman became President
	1946	**Matthew Henson** was honored by the U.S. Navy
	1950	the Korean War began
chosen to be an astronaut	**1959**	
rocketed into space	**1961**	**Jacqueline Cochran** flew at twice the speed of sound
	1962	John Glenn orbited the Earth
	1969	Neil Armstrong stepped on the Moon
flew to the Moon on Apollo 14	**1971**	
resigned from the astronaut program and the Navy	**1974**	
	1975	the Vietnam War ended
	1992	Bill Clinton was elected President
died at the age of 75	**1998**	Senator John Glenn returned to space in the shuttle *Discovery*

Research:

www.jsc.nasa.gov/Bios/htmlbios/shepard-alan.html

Matthew Henson

1866–1955

Matthew Henson was born in 1866. His parents died in 1877 when he was still a child. Young Matthew decided to get a job on a ship. He walked all the way from Washington, D.C., to Baltimore, Maryland. A ship captain gave him a job as a cabin boy. The ship traveled all around the world. Matthew was only 12 years old, but he was already on a great adventure.

In 1891 Matthew began the greatest adventure of his life. He joined another explorer, Robert Peary, on a trip to Greenland. Peary wanted to be the first man to reach the North Pole. He asked Matthew to be his assistant. For the next twenty years, they made many trips to Greenland, drawing maps and making trails.

On March 1, 1909, they were ready to go all the way. It was a long and dangerous trip. They both reached the North Pole, but only Peary was given an award. Finally, in 1946, the U.S. Navy gave Matthew a medal for his Arctic explorations. He also got a gold medal from the Chicago Geographic Society. Matthew Henson died in 1955, at the age of 89. He is buried in the Arlington National Cemetery, next to many other American heroes.

TIMELINE

Matthew Henson		America
was born in Charles County, Maryland, to free African American parents	**1866**	the Ku Klux Klan was formed
	1870	the U.S. Weather Bureau was founded
parents died	**1877**	
was hired as a cabin boy on a ship	**1878**	
	1889	**A. Philip Randolph** was born; **Nellie Bly** went around the world
joined Robert Peary on a trip to Greenland	**1891**	
	1898	the U.S. took Puerto Rico in the Spanish-American War
Henson and Peary and several Inuit made it to the North Pole	**1909**	
	1911	the first transcontinental airplane flight
	1915	the first transcontinental telephone call
	1920	Robert Peary died
the Navy gave Matthew an award for his Arctic explorations	**1946**	
	1953	Dwight Eisenhower became President
died at the age of 89	**1955**	Rosa Parks began the Montgomery bus boycott with **M.L. King, Jr.**

Research:
www.matthewhenson.org

Sacagawea

1786–1812

Sacagawea was a member of the Shoshone tribe. She was probably born around 1786. In the 1780s, the Shoshone were at war with the Hidatsa, another tribe. One day, the Hidatsa kidnapped Sacagawea. She was just 14 years old. The Hidatsa took her from her home in Idaho to live with them in North Dakota. Then she was sold as a slave to a French Canadian fur trapper, Charbonneau.

In 1804 two white men came to their village. Their names were Meriwether Lewis and William Clark. They had 40 other men with them. The President of the United States had asked them to find a route all the way to the Pacific Ocean. Lewis and Clark asked Sacagawea to help them find their way. They thought she would be helpful when they came to the land of the Shoshone people in Montana and Idaho. She agreed, and they left in the spring, Sacagawea carrying her baby on her back.

Sacagawea guided the group through the forests and mountains. She was the only woman in the whole group. Her language skills helped them communicate with other Native Americans. However, Sacagawea did not speak English. Her husband Charbonneau spoke Hidatsa with Sacagawea and Charbonneau spoke French to one of the explorers who translated the original message into English for Lewis and Clark.

They finally reached Oregon and the Pacific Ocean in the late fall of 1805. Sacagawea had helped to connect two different parts of the country. She returned to North Dakota in 1806 and died there in 1812.

TIMELINE

Sacagawea		America
was born in a Shoshone village	**1786**	
	1799	**George Washington** died
was kidnapped by the Hidatsa	**1800**	the U.S. government moved to Washington, D.C.
	1801	Thomas Jefferson became President
	1803	the U.S. bought the Louisiana territory
met Meriwether Lewis and William Clark	**1804**	Jefferson sent Lewis and Clark to explore the Louisiana Purchase
helped Lewis and Clark find their way to the Pacific Ocean	**1805**	the U.S. Navy and Marines defeated the Barbary Pirates near Tripoli in North Africa
returned to North Dakota	**1806**	
	1807	Fulton ran a steamboat from New York City to Albany
	1809	Lewis committed suicide **Abraham Lincoln** was born
gave birth to a daughter died at the age of 26	**1812**	the U.S. went to war with Britain
	1813	Clark adopted Sacagawea's children

Research:
www.PBS.org/lewisandclark/inside/saca.html

Martin Luther King, Jr.

1929–1968

Martin Luther King, Jr. was born on January 15, 1929. His family was very religious. He studied sociology and religion and got a Ph.D. from Boston University. His dream was to help the poor. He especially wanted to help other African Americans.

Dr. King taught his followers to stand up for their rights. But he also told them not to use violence. In 1963 he was put in jail for leading a protest. Still, he continued to fight for justice. In 1964 he received the Nobel Peace Prize.

Martin Luther King, Jr. also had many enemies. An assassin killed him on April 4, 1968.

A

TIMELINE

Martin Luther King, Jr.		America
was born on January 15	**1929**	the Stock Market crashed
	1936	Jessie Owens won 4 gold medals at the Berlin Olympics **Franklin Delano Roosevelt** was elected President
	1937	Joe Lewis became Heavyweight Boxing Champion of the World
became a minister	**1946**	
	1947	Jackie Robinson broke the "color barrier" in baseball
	1954	the Supreme Court ruled that racial segregation in public schools is illegal
was one of leaders of the Montgomery bus boycott started by Rosa Parks	**1955**	**Roberto Clemente** began his baseball career with the Pittsburgh Pirates
was jailed for leading a protest	**1963**	The March on Washingon
received the Nobel Peace Prize	**1964**	
	1965	Malcolm X was assassinated **Cesar Chavez** organized a strike
was assassinated	**1968**	

Research:

seattletimes.nwsource.com/mlk

Susan B. Anthony

1820 –1906

Susan B. Anthony was born on February 15, 1820. She became a school-teacher when she was 17 years old. She earned $2.50 per week. But male teachers earned $10 per week. Susan thought this was unfair. She thought women and men should make the same amount of money.

Susan also thought women should have the right to vote. In 1872 she tried to vote in a presidential election, but she was arrested. A judge ordered her to pay $100, but she refused. Instead, she demanded the right to vote. She traveled around the country, giving speeches. She even spoke to President Theodore Roosevelt.

Susan B. Anthony died on March 13, 1906. At the time, only four states allowed women to vote. In 1920 Congress passed the 19th Amendment to the Constitution. It is known as the "Susan B. Anthony Amendment," because it gave all women in the United States the right to vote.

TIMELINE

Susan B. Anthony		America
was born February 15 in Adams, Massachusetts	**1820**	
	1821	the first college for women opened in Troy, N.Y.
became a teacher; was active against slavery and for temperance (anti-alcohol)	**1837**	
	1842	settlers moved west on the Oregon Trail
	1844	**Sarah Winnemucca** was born
was arrested for trying to vote demanded the right to vote (women's suffrage)	**1872**	
	1890	the poems of **Emily Dickinson** were published
	1901	Theodore Roosevelt became President
died on March 13	**1906**	San Francisco was hit by an earthquake
	1914	**Nellie Bly** reported on WWI
	1916	Jeannette Rankin was elected the first female member of the U.S. House of Representatives
	1920	the 19th Amendment was passed, giving women the right to vote
the Susan B. Anthony dollar was issued	**1979**	

Research:

www.womenshistory.about.com/library/bio/blanthony.htm

Princess Kaiulani

1875–1899

Kaiulani Lunalilo was a Hawaiian princess. She was born on October 16, 1875. When she was fourteen, the King and Queen sent her to a boarding school in England, where she studied languages and history.

While Kaiulani was in England, the King died. The new Queen tried to preserve Hawaii's independence. American businessmen in Hawaii had become very powerful. They owned most of the land, and they wanted to make Hawaii a U.S. territory. In January of 1893, U.S. Marines landed on the island to back up the American businessmen. The Queen was locked up, and a Republic was declared.

In February, Kaiulani spoke to reporters about the injustice of this invasion. Then she went to Washington, D.C. to meet with President Grover Cleveland. The President was convinced by Kaiulani's speech. He told Congress to restore Hawaii's independence. But the American businessmen in Hawaii refused to give up their power.

Princess Kaiulani returned to Hawaii in 1897, the same year that President Cleveland left office. American troops in Hawaii then took total control of the island. Princess Kaiulani was heartbroken. She died of a fever on March 6, 1899. She was only 23 years old. Hawaii officially became a U.S. territory the following year.

C 204 words

TIMELINE

Princess Kaiulani		America
was born October 16 in Honolulu; her mother was the king's sister; her father was Scottish	**1875**	
	1882	the U.S. Congress barred Chinese immigration
	1886	the Statue of Liberty was opened
was sent to an English boarding school	**1889**	
	1890	**Duke Kahanamoku** was born
	1891	the king died Kaiulani's aunt became Queen Lili'uokalani, the last Hawaiian ruler
U.S. Marines landed in Hawaii and overthrew the Queen came to the U.S. to plead for her people's liberty Hawaii was declared a republic	**1893**	Grover Cleveland became President, met with and encouraged Kaiulani, and refused to accept annexation of Hawaii
returned to Hawaii	**1897**	William McKinley became President
	1898	the U.S. annexed Hawaii and took Guam and Puerto Rico
died of a fever on March 6	**1899**	
	1900	Hawaii became a U.S. territory
	1949	Hawaii became a state

Research:

www.hawaiischoolreports.com/history/kaiulani.htm

Level C   54   **Human Rights Leaders**

Sarah Winnemucca

1844–1891

Sarah Winnemucca was a Paiute Indian. She was born in what is now Nevada. When she was young, the U.S. government forced the Paiutes to leave their native lands, and the family was broken up. In 1857 Sarah was adopted by a white family. She learned how to read and write English. Her early experiences taught her how to move between these two cultures.

In 1866 Sarah moved back to Nevada. She lived on an Indian reservation with her brother, Natchez. The Paiutes were plotting a war against U.S. troops. Sarah wanted to avoid the war, because she knew that many Paiutes would be killed. She helped to negotiate a peace treaty between the Paiutes and the U.S. army. After that, the army asked Sarah to work for them as an interpreter. From 1867 to 1868, Sarah worked for the U.S. Army at Fort McDermit, in Nevada.

Sarah became a spokesperson for the Paiutes and other Native American tribes. In 1879 she gave a series of lectures in San Francisco about the problems of Native Americans. The Paiutes had been forced off their native lands and had nowhere to go. Sarah went as far as Washington, D.C. to raise money for the Paiutes. To raise more money, she wrote a book in 1883 called *Life Among the Paiutes*. In 1890 Sarah moved to Montana to be close to her brother and sister. She died there in 1891, after a life of service to her people.

TIMELINE

Sarah Winnemucca		America
was born in Nevada	**1844**	
	1847	the Mormons established Salt Lake City, Utah
	1848	gold was discovered in California
was adopted by a white family	**1857**	
	1861	**Lincoln** became President and the Civil War began
moved to an Indian reservation in Nevada	**1866**	
interpreted for the U.S. Army	**1867**	Alaska was sold to the U.S.
	1876	**Chief Joseph** refused to give Nez Perce land to the U.S.
gave lectures in San Francisco	**1879**	
wrote *Life Among the Paiutes*	**1883**	Buffalo Bill started his Wild West Show
	1884	**Mark Twain** wrote *Huckleberry Finn*
moved to Montana	**1890**	**Sitting Bull** was killed while being arrested
died at the age of 47	**1891**	

Research:

www.powersource.com/gallery/womansp/paiute.html

Andrew Carnegie

1835–1919

Andrew Carnegie was born in Scotland in 1835. He came to the U.S. with his family in 1848. Young Andrew got a job as a messenger. He saved money and invested in a railroad company. He continued to make very good business decisions. In 1865 he began developing the steel industry in Pittsburgh. By 1901 Andrew Carnegie was the richest man in the world.

In 1902 he started the Carnegie Foundation. He used his fortune to support education, research, and world peace. Carnegie died seventeen years later. But his programs still exist. They have given hundreds of millions of dollars to universities, libraries, and other organizations.

TIMELINE

Andrew Carnegie		America
was born in Scotlnd	**1835**	
moved to the U.S. with his family	**1848**	
	1859	the first oil well in Pennsylvania was drilled
began investing in steel	**1865**	
	1869	the Transcontinental Railroad was completed
	1870	John D. Rockefeller started the Standard Oil Company
	1882	the Brooklyn Bridge was built
	1889	**A. Philip Randolph** was born
became the richest man in the world	**1901**	
started the Carnegie Foundation	**1902**	
	1913	Woodrow Wilson became President
	1917	**John F. Kennedy** was born
died on August 11	**1919**	WWI ended at 11 a.m. on 11/11

Research:

www.pbs.org/wgbh/amex/carnegie/peopleevents/pande01.html

Cesar Chavez

1927–1993

Cesar Chavez was born in 1927 in Arizona. His mother and father were farmers. But in the 1930s, there was a terrible drought in the United States. The Chavez family could not pay their taxes. They lost their farm in 1937. The family had to travel from place to place, looking for work.

The life of migrant farm workers was very difficult. They worked in the hot sun all day. They made a dollar an hour. Some landowners subtracted money for the water they drank. In 1952 Cesar began to organize the migrant workers to improve their working conditions.

In 1965 Cesar organized a strike in California. In 1971 he helped to organize the United Farm Workers of America (UFW). He also fasted as a form of protest. In 1988 he didn't eat anything for 36 days in a row. Weakened from so much work and fasting, Cesar Chavez died in 1993.

TIMELINE

Cesar Chavez		America
was born on March 31 in Arizona	**1927**	
	1930s	the Great Economic Depression began and continued
the family lost their farm	**1937**	
	1941	the U.S. joined World War II
	1944	**William Kenzo Nakamura** was killed
became a community organizer	**1952**	
	1962	**Rachel Carson's** *Silent Spring* was published
	1963	Lyndon Johnson became President
	1964	Congress enacted Johnson's "War on Poverty"
organized a strike in California	**1965**	
helped start the United Farm Workers of America	**1971**	
	1972	**Roberto Clemente** was killed in an airplane crash
fasted for 38 days	**1988**	
died	**1993**	

Research:

www.americaslibrary.gov/cgi-bin/page.cgi/aa/chavez

Mother Jones

1830–1930

Mary Harris was born in Ireland in 1830. She came to the United States when she was five years old. In 1861 she married George Jones, an iron worker in Memphis, Tennessee. Mr. and Mrs. Jones had four children, all of them boys.

In 1867 tragedy struck the Jones family. An epidemic of yellow fever hit Memphis. Mr. Jones and his four sons caught the disease. Tragically, they all died in the same week.

Mary didn't want to stay in Memphis, so she moved to Chicago. She started a sewing business, but tragedy struck again. In 1871 a great fire burned the city of Chicago. Mary lost everything she owned. Not knowing what to do, she asked a labor union for help. Through the union, Mary learned about the problems of other workers. She found out that many workers were overworked and underpaid. In 1877 she helped to organize a strike at a railroad company. It was one of the first strikes in American history.

Mary continued to fight for workers' rights. People called her "Mother Jones" because of her white hair. She lived to be 100 years old, and was very active even in her later years.

TIMELINE

Mother Jones		America
Mary Harris was born in Ireland	**1830**	
came to the United States	**1835**	
married George Jones	**1861**	**Abraham Lincoln** became President
	1865	the steel industry was developed by **Andrew Carnegie**
Mr. Jones and his four sons died	**1867**	
lost everything in the fire	**1871**	Chicago was destroyed by fire
organized a strike at the railroad company	**1877**	President Hayes sent troops to break up the railroad strike
	1925	the Railroad Porters Union was organized by **A. Philip Randolph**
	1927	**Cesar Chavez** was born
	1929	Herbert Hoover became President the Stock Market crashed
died at the age of 100	**1930**	Depression became worldwide; the Hoover administration tried to help high U.S. unemployment by deporting Mexican laborers.

Research:

www.kentlaw.edu/ilhs/majones.htm

A. Philip Randolph

1889–1979

Asa Philip Randolph was born in Florida in 1889. In 1911 he moved to Harlem, a neighborhood in New York City where many other African Americans lived. The next year, he enrolled in the City College of New York and became politically active. At the time, the United States was at war. He spoke out against the war, and he was arrested for giving an anti-war speech in 1918.

After the war, Randolph concentrated on the problems of African American workers. In those days, only certain jobs were open to African Americans. Most of these jobs were service positions. Porters, for example, served food and carried bags on trains. But they hardly made enough money to pay for their own basic needs. In 1925 Asa became president of the Brotherhood of Sleeping Car Porters. The Brotherhood was a labor union, and it negotiated better working conditions for porters.

Randolph continued to fight for the rights of African American workers throughout his life. He organized many protests and marches. In 1963 he gave a famous speech at the Lincoln Memorial in Washington, D.C. He asked the nation to make good jobs available to all Americans who were willing to work hard. He called this a "revolution for jobs and freedom." The following year, President Lyndon B. Johnson gave Randolph the Medal of Freedom — the nation's highest honor to an American citizen.

Randolph resigned as president of the Brotherhood of Sleeping Car Porters in 1968, and he died in 1979 at the age of 90.

TIMELINE

A. Philip Randolph		America
was born in Florida on April 15	**1889**	
moved to Harlem, New York City	**1891**	**Zora Neale Hurston** was born
	1911	the Erie Canal was opened
enrolled in the City College of New York	**1912**	
	1917	the U.S. declared war on Germany
was arrested for giving an anti-war speech	**1918**	
became president of the Brotherhood of Sleeping Car Porters	**1925**	
	1930	**Mother Jones** died
	1933	Congress passed the "New Deal"
	1935	the CIO (Union) was formed
gave a famous speech calling for "revolution"	**1963**	**Jack Kennedy** was assassinated
received the Medal of Freedom from President Johnson	**1964**	
resigned as president of the Brotherhood of Sleeping Car Porters	**1968**	**Martin Luther King, Jr.** was killed Robert Kennedy was killed
died at the age of 90 on May 16	**1979**	

Research:
www.philsch.k12.pa.us/schools/randolph/A_P_Randolph.html

George Washington

1732–1799

George Washington was born in 1732. He was an American colonist and military officer for Britain's army in America. He served the British in a war against the French in 1754. Britain and the colonists won the war.

In 1775 the colonists began their fight for independence from Great Britain. The colonists chose Washington to be the commander-in-chief. The colonies declared their independence in 1776. The Revolutionary War finally ended in 1781. Under Washington's leadership, the new American nation won the war. The American Congress chose Washington as the first President of the United States in 1789. Four years later, he was elected again. Washington died in 1799. Today he is known as the "father of his country."

TIMELINE

George Washington		America
was born on February 22 in Virginia	**1732**	Ben Franklin first published *Poor Richard's Almanac*
served as a leader in a war against the French	**1754**	
married Martha Custis	**1759**	the French colony of Quebec fell to the British
was chosen to be commander-in-chief of the colonial army	**1775**	the Battle of Lexington and Concord began the fight for independence **Daniel Boone** built the Wilderness Road
	1776	the colonies declared their independence on July 4
	1780	the French army arrived to help the Americans
	1781	the British surrendered at Yorktown
became the first U. S. President	**1789**	
	1792	**John Paul Jones** died in Paris
was elected President for a second time	**1793**	
	1797	John Adams became President
died on December 14	**1799**	

Research:

www.whitehouse.gov/history/presidents/gw1.html

Abraham Lincoln

1809–1865

Abraham Lincoln was born on a farm in Kentucky. In 1816 the family moved to Indiana, and in 1830 Lincoln moved to Illinois, where he became a lawyer and senator.

Lincoln was good at giving speeches, and he spoke out against slavery. The problem of slavery had divided the country. Lincoln convinced voters he could lead them to a solution. In 1860 he was elected President of the United States. But slavery continued to divide the country. In 1861 ten states withdrew from the union and the Civil War started.

Lincoln was reelected in 1864, while the country was still at war with itself. In January of 1865, Lincoln added the 13th Amendment to the Constitution, ending slavery. The South surrendered on April 9th. Five days after the war ended, Lincoln went to the theater. During the play, he was shot and killed by John Wilkes Booth. The country had lost one of its greatest leaders.

TIMELINE

Abraham Lincoln		America
was born on a farm in Kentucky	**1809**	
	1810	the U.S. population was 7.2 million
the family moved to Indiana	**1816**	
	1821	**Clara Barton** was born
	1824	slavery was abolished in Illinois
moved to Illinois	**1830**	
	1850	California became the 31st state
was elected the 16th President of the U.S.	**1860**	**Nellie Bly** was born
	1861	the Civil War began
was reelected	**1864**	
(January) abolished slavery in the U.S. with the 13th Amendment	**1865**	(April 9th) the South surrendered, ending the Civil War
(April 14) was shot and killed by John Wilkes Booth		
	1870	**Robert E. Lee** died

Research:
www.whitehouse.gov/history/presidents/al16.html

Franklin Delano Roosevelt

1882–1945

Franklin Delano Roosevelt was born in 1882. He grew up in Hyde Park, New York. His family was wealthy, and Franklin received an excellent education.

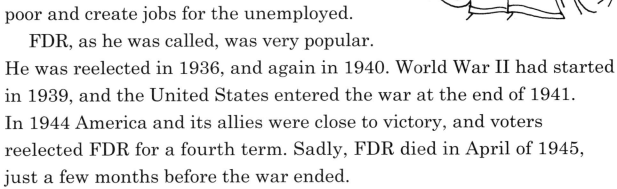

Franklin entered politics in 1913. But in 1921, he caught polio and could no longer walk. He was determined to fight this disease. He swam regularly to get back his health. In 1928 he was strong enough to enter politics once again. In that year, he was elected governor of New York, even though he still had to use leg braces and a cane.

Hard times hit the country in the 1930s. Many Americans lost their homes and their jobs. Roosevelt proposed some new ideas for overcoming the crisis, and he was elected President in 1932. He started public programs called the "New Deal" to help the poor and create jobs for the unemployed.

FDR, as he was called, was very popular. He was reelected in 1936, and again in 1940. World War II had started in 1939, and the United States entered the war at the end of 1941. In 1944 America and its allies were close to victory, and voters reelected FDR for a fourth term. Sadly, FDR died in April of 1945, just a few months before the war ended.

TIMELINE

Franklin Roosevelt		America
was born in Hyde Park, New York	**1882**	**Jane Addams** opened Hull House
	1901	Theodore Roosevelt became President
entered politics	**1913**	
	1917	the U.S. entered World War I
caught polio	**1921**	**William Kenzo Nakamura** was born in Seattle
reentered politics	**1928**	
	1929	the stock market crashed
was elected President	**1932**	**Amelia Earhart** flew the Atlantic
	1933	Congress passed the "New Deal"
was elected President for the second time	**1936**	
	1939	World War II began in Europe
	1942	the U.S. moved Japanese Americans to detention camps
was elected President for the fourth time	**1944**	
died in April	**1945**	nuclear bombs were dropped on Japan Japan surrendered on August 14

Research:

www.whitehouse.gov/history/presidents/fr32.html

John F. Kennedy

1917–1963

John F. "Jack" Kennedy was born in Massachusetts in 1917. He joined the U.S. Navy in 1941, right after the United States entered World War II. Kennedy was a boat commander in the Pacific Ocean. One night, his boat was bombed, and Kennedy and the crew swam to a nearby island. He towed a man who was badly burned all the way to the island. Kennedy saved his crewman's life, but his back was injured, and he had to be hospitalized. Later, he received a medal for "outstanding courage, endurance, and leadership."

After the war, Kennedy decided to enter politics. He was elected to the House of Representatives in 1946, and in 1952 he became a senator. Shortly after that, he had an operation on his back, and had to spend a lot of time in bed. While he was resting, he wrote *Profiles in Courage*, a book about American senators who had followed their conscience. It won the Pulitzer Prize in 1957.

In 1960 JFK was elected President of the United States. Kennedy's presidency was an exciting but sometimes dangerous time. He started the Peace Corps in 1961 to help developing countries. But a year later, he came very close to declaring war on the Soviet Union. And in 1963 Kennedy presented a Civil Rights Bill to Congress. Unfortunately, he did not live to see his bill become law. He was shot and killed during a parade on November 22, 1963.

TIMELINE

John F. Kennedy		America
was born in Brookline, Massachusetts	**1917**	
	1929	**Roosevelt** was elected President
joined the U.S. Navy	**1941**	the U.S. entered World War II
elected to the U.S. House of Representatives	**1946**	
elected to the U.S. Senate	**1952**	
	1955	**Martin Luther King, Jr.** helped organize the Montgomery, Alabama, bus boycott
won the Pulitzer Prize	**1957**	
	1958	the first jet airline route was opened from New York to Miami
elected President	**1960**	**Zora Neale Hurston** died in poverty
started the Peace Corps	**1961**	
	1962	the Russians sent missiles to Cuba
was assassinated in Dallas	**1963**	Lyndon Johnson became President
	1964	Congress passed the Civil Rights Act

Research:

www.www.whitehouse.gov/history/presidents/jk35.html

Robert E. Lee

1807–1870

Robert E. Lee was born in 1807. He grew up on a farm in Virginia. In 1829 he went to the West Point Military Academy. Lee then became a lieutenant in the U.S. Army. From 1846 to 1848, Lieutenant Lee served in the war with Mexico. He continued his career in the U.S. Army until 1861.

In 1861 the Civil War began when the southern slave states separated from the United States. Lee's home state of Virginia was a slave state, but Lee was against slavery. However, he did not want to fight against his fellow Virginians. So he became a general for the Confederacy. General Lee was a brilliant leader, but in 1865 he admitted defeat and surrendered to General Ulysses S. Grant. Lee died five years later in 1870.

TIMELINE

Robert E. Lee		America
was born on January 19 in Virginia	**1807**	
	1809	**Abraham Lincoln** was born James Monroe became President
went to West Point Military Academy	**1829**	
	1846	the Mexican War began
served in the war with Mexico	**1846-1848**	gold was discovered in California
became a Confederate general	**1861**	the Civil War began (July) the South defeated the North in the first major battle of the war at Bull Run
	1863	Confederates surrendered Vicksburg and lost the Battle of Gettysburg
	1864	General Sherman took Atlanta
surrendered to General U.S. Grant	**1865**	**Lincoln** was assassinated
served as president of Washington College (now Washington and Lee University)	**1865-1870**	**Andrew Carnegie** invested in steel (1869) Grant became President
died on October 12	**1870**	

Research:

www.civilwarhome.com/leebio.htm

John Paul Jones

1747–1792

John Paul Jones was born in Scotland in 1747. He went to sea on a ship at the age of thirteen. At 21 he became the commander of his own ship. After several years, he immigrated to the British colonies in North America.

In 1775 the colonies revolted against Great Britain. The colonists chose John Paul Jones to be the commander of the Continental Navy. Jones sailed to England in September of 1779. He fought a fierce battle with British forces in his ship *Bonhomme Richard* and won. His ship was badly damaged. It sank the day after the battle.

The colonies won their independence from Great Britain in 1783. The Continental Navy was now the U.S. Navy. In 1788 Jones went to Europe, served in the Russian navy for a while, and died in Paris in 1792. His body was brought back to the United States more than 100 years later, in 1913, and laid to rest in a U.S. Naval cemetery in Maryland.

B 165 words

TIMELINE

John Paul Jones		America
was born in Scotland on July 6	**1747**	
went to sea	**1760**	New France surrendered to Britain
became commander of his own ship	**1768**	
	1773	the "Boston Tea Party" protested British taxes
was chosen to command the Continental Navy	**1775**	the colonies revolted **Washington** took command of the Continental Army in Boston **Daniel Boone** built Boonesboro
	1778	France sent ships to support the Americans
	1779	
fought and won a major battle with British forces at sea	**1783**	the colonies won their independence
served in the Russian navy	**1788**	
died in Paris, July 18	**1792**	
	1797	**Washington** retired to Mt. Vernon John Adams became President
was moved to the U.S. was buried in Maryland	**1913**	

Research:

www.chinfo.navy.mil/navpalib/traditions/html/jpjones.html

Jacqueline Cochran

1910–1980

Jacqueline Cochran was born in Pensacola, Florida. She became an orphan at an early age and grew up in poverty. Jacqueline got her first job at the age of eight, and she continued to work very hard. Eventually, she started her own cosmetics company. To advertise her business, she learned how to fly. She thought this was a good way to get people's attention. In 1932 "Jackie" obtained her license to fly.

Jackie became more and more interested in airplanes and flying. She gave up her cosmetics business and became a full-time aviator. In 1938 she set a speed record for women flying across North America.

When the United States entered World War II in 1941, Cochran was appointed director of the Women's Air Force Service Pilots. She trained women to fly warplanes across the Atlantic to the U.S. Army Air Force in Europe. She herself was the first woman to fly a bomber across the ocean.

After the war, Cochran continued to break world records. In 1953, she broke the world speed record for both men and women. And in 1961, she became the first woman to fly at twice the speed of sound. Jacqueline broke more records than any other aviator. She died in 1980, at the age of 70.

C 212 words TIMELINE

Jacqueline Cochran		America
was born in Pensacola, Florida	**1910**	
got her first job	**1918**	
	1927	Lindbergh flew solo across the Atlantic Ocean
obtained her license to fly	**1932**	
	1937	**Amelia Earhart** disappeared in the Pacific
set a speed record for women flying across North America	**1938**	
trained women pilots during World War II	**1941- 1945**	(1942) B-17s and B-24s began bombing Germany
	1944	D-Day; Allied forces landed in Europe
broke the world speed record for both men and women	**1953**	
became the first woman to fly at twice the speed of sound	**1961**	Alan Shepard became the first American in space
	1962	**John Glenn** orbited the Earth
died at the age of 70	**1980**	

Research:

www.wasp-wwii.org/wasp/jacqueline_cochran.htm

William Kenzo Nakamura

1921–1944

William Kenzo Nakamura was born in 1921 in Seattle, Washington. His parents had immigrated to the United States from Japan before he was born. At home, he was called "Kenzo," but his classmates called him "Bill."

Kenzo graduated from high school in 1939, and enrolled in the University of Washington to study medicine. But tragedy interrupted his studies. The United States declared war on Japan in 1941, and his mother died shortly after. Two months later, Kenzo and the rest of his family were sent to an internment camp in Idaho.

Unfortunately, the U.S. government did not trust Japanese American citizens. It sent them to internment camps as a form of imprisonment. These American citizens could not leave the camps, and they had no rights. In spite of this injustice, Kenzo decided that he wanted to serve his country. He enlisted in the U.S. Army and was shipped to Italy in 1943.

On the fourth of July, 1944, his platoon came under fire. Kenzo fought bravely while his comrades moved to safety. Through his bravery, Kenzo saved his entire platoon. Unfortunately, Kenzo was shot and killed. He was laid to rest at a cemetery in Seattle.

After the war Japanese Americans held at internment camps were released. None of them had been found guilty of any crime against the United States. But it took the government some time to honor the Japanese-Americans who had served in the war. In 2000 William Kenzo Nakamura finally received a Congressional Medal of Honor for his heroism during World War II.

TIMELINE

W. Kenzo Nakamura		America
was born in Seattle, Washington	**1921**	
	1932	the world was in Depression **Franklin Roosevelt** was elected President
graduated from high school enrolled in the University of Washington	**1939**	
	1940	**Bruce Lee** was born California
	1941	Japanese airplanes bombed Pearl Harbor in Hawaii the U.S. declared war on Japan
Kenzo's mother died family imprisoned in an internment camp in Idaho	**1942**	the U.S. was forced to surrender the Philippines to Japan
was sent to Italy	**1943**	American and British forces landed in Italy **Jack Kennedy's** PT 109 was sunk
(July 4) saved his platoon was shot and killed	**1944**	the Allies invaded Normandy on D-Day
received the Congressional Medal of Honor	**2000**	

Research:

www.historylink.org/output.cfm?file_id=2767

Mark Twain

1835–1910

Mark Twain was born in 1835. His real name was Samuel Clemens. He grew up in a small town near the Mississippi River. In 1850 he got a job as a journalist. He traveled all over the world. His travel essays became very popular. In 1863 he adopted the name "Mark Twain."

In 1876 Twain wrote a novel called *The Adventures of Tom Sawyer*. It told about a boy's life in a Mississippi River town. Eight years later, he wrote a novel about Tom Sawyer's friend. It was called *The Adventures of Huckleberry Finn*.

Twain wrote about serious issues, but with humor. He died in 1910, but Mark Twain lives on through his wonderful books.

TIMELINE

Mark Twain		America
was born on November 30 as Samuel Clemens	**1835**	
	1848	gold was discovered in California
got a job as a journalist traveled around the world	**1850**	
	1861	the Civil War began
adopted the name "Mark Twain"	**1863**	
wrote *The Adventures of Tom Sawyer*	**1876**	Custer lost the Battle of the Little Bighorn
wrote *The Adventures of Huckleberry Finn*	**1884**	
	1885	**Nellie Bly** became a journalist and author
	1886	**Emily Dickinson** died
wrote *A Connecticut Yankee in King Arthur's Court*	**1889**	
	1900	**Frank Baum's** *The Wonderful Wizard of Oz* was published
	1901	Theodore Roosevelt became President
	1907	*The Life and Adventures of* **Nat Love** was published
died on April 21	**1910**	

Research:
www.geocities.com/swaisman

Emily Dickinson

1830–1886

Emily Dickinson was born in Amherst, Massachusetts, in 1830. She lived in the same house her whole life. Her family was wealthy, so Emily did not have to work, and she never married.

Emily started to write poems when she was about 20 years old. She created her own books by sewing pages together with needle and thread. People thought that she was strange. She spent most of her time in her room and always dressed in white.

Emily lived a very private life. She kept her thoughts and feelings to herself. She wrote hundreds of poems. But, in her lifetime, she published only seven of them. After Emily's death in 1886, her sister discovered her poems. She published a book of the poems in 1891. It took many years to organize and publish the rest of Dickinson's work. The last book, called *Bolts of Melody*, was published in 1945. She has been called "perhaps the greatest woman poet since Sappho."

TIMELINE

Emily Dickinson		America
was born in Amherst, Massachusetts	**1830**	
	1831	Westbrook Seminary, first co-ed boarding school, was chartered
	1833	Oberlin College admitted women
	1835	**Mark Twain** was born
	1837	**Susan B. Anthony** began teaching
	1841	Edgar Allan Poe's *Murders in the Rue Morgue* was published
began to write poetry	**1850**	English poet Elizabeth Browning, much admired by Emily, wrote *Sonnets from the Portuguese*
	1851	Melville's *Moby Dick* was published
	1852	Harriet Beecher Stowe wrote *Uncle Tom's Cabin*
	1861	**Clara Barton** became a nurse Julia Ward Howe's *Battle Hymn of the Republic* was published
	1884	*Huckleberry Finn* was published
	1886	
died on May 15 in Amherst	**1891**	
Emily's sister published a book of her poems	**1945**	
Bolts of Melody was published		

Research:

www.poets.org/poet.php/prmPID/155

Zora Neale Hurston

1891 –1960

Zora Neale Hurston was born in Eatonville, Florida, in 1891. She was a talented storyteller and writer. In 1919 Zora enrolled at Howard University, an African American university in Washington, D.C. Zora got a degree in anthropology, specializing in folklore.

In 1927 Hurston went back to Florida. She traveled all around the South, collecting African American folklore, jokes, and traditional sayings. These "tall tales" were published in a book called *Mules and Men*, in 1932.

In 1937 Hurston wrote a novel called *Their Eyes Were Watching God*. It was about the lives of southern African Americans, and it showed how they really talked. Many people did not like it, but Zora pursued this style of writing. She wanted to write about real people in the real world.

Zora sometimes traveled to the Caribbean. Her fourth book, *Tell My Horse,* was published in 1938. It tells about her travels in Haiti and Jamaica. In this book, Zora was able to combine her interests in anthropology and folklore.

Money was a problem throughout Zora's life. To make enough money to live on, she even worked as a maid. She died in 1960 at a welfare home and was buried in an unmarked grave.

201 words

TIMELINE

Zora Neal Hurston		America
was born in Eatonville, Florida	**1891**	
	1894	**Edison's** motion picture was shown
	1899	Scott Joplin's "Maple Leaf Rag" was published
	1915	the U.S. occupied Haiti (until 1934)
enrolled at Howard University	**1919**	
	1920	the 19th amendment gave women the right to vote
went back to Florida	**1927**	
	1928	**Amelia Earhart** flew acoss the Atlantic
wrote *Mules and Men*	**1932**	
	1935	George Gershwin's *Porgy and Bess* opened
wrote *Their Eyes Were Watching God*	**1937**	
wrote *Tell My Horse*	**1938**	the national minimum wage was established
	1940	Richard Wright's *Native Son* was published
died at a welfare home buried in an unmarked grave	**1960**	

Research:

www.lkwdpl.org/wihohio/hurs-zor.htm

L. Frank Baum

1856–1919

Lyman Frank Baum was born in Chittenango, New York. He preferred to be called Frank, so he used only an initial for his first name. In his early years, Baum tried a variety of careers. In 1873 he became a journalist for *The New York World*. He followed that with a brief career as an actor. He even wrote his own plays and owned his own theater.

In 1897 Baum tried his hand at writing with a novel called *Mother Goose in Prose.* Baum said he wanted to create modern fairy tales and not scare children like the Brothers Grimm. In 1899 Baum wrote a book of poems for children. It was called *Father Goose,* and it was very popular. Then in 1900, he wrote a novel for young readers. It was called *The Wonderful Wizard of Oz.* In it, a young girl named Dorothy is swept away by a cyclone to a magical land where she experiences amazing adventures with fascinating characters.

The Wonderful Wizard of Oz was successful, and so Baum turned it into a series, writing *Ozma of Oz* (1907), *The Road to Oz* (1909), and *Tik-Tok of Oz* (1914) among others. All in all, Baum wrote 62 books, most of them for children.

L. Frank Baum died in 1919, while he was working on *Glinda of Oz*, and it was published the following year. Other writers have helped to continue the series since then. In 1939 the film version *of The Wonderful Wizard of Oz* was produced. It was nominated for an Academy Award, and it is now a classic film known all around the world.

TIMELINE

L. Frank Baum		America
was born in Chittenango, New York, on May 15	**1856**	The first kindergarten in the U. S. was opened
became a journalist	**1873**	
Father Goose was published	**1891**	**Dickinson's** poetry was published
The Wonderful Wizard of Oz was published	**1900**	**Booker T. Washington** wrote *Up from Slavery*
	1901	**Zora Neale Hurston** was born
	1903	the Wright Brothers' airplane flew at Kitty Hawk, North Carolina
Ozma of Oz was published	**1907**	
The Road to Oz was published	**1909**	
	1912	the Girl Scouts was founded
Tik-Tok of Oz was published	**1914**	
died on May 6th	**1919**	
Glinda of Oz was published	**1920**	**Amelia Earhart** started to fly
	1927	*The Jazz Singer,* first successful sound film, was released
	1939	The first successful color films, *The Wizard of Oz* and *Gone with the Wind*, were released

Research:
en.wikipedia.org/wiki/L._Frank_Baum

Marian Anderson

1897–1993

Marian Anderson was born in Philadelphia in 1897. She loved to sing.
In 1923 Marian won first prize at a singing contest. The next year, she
gave a recital in New York City. After that she sang and traveled all
around the world.

Marian sometimes experienced prejudice. In 1939 the owners of a
music hall did not let her sing because of her color. Eleanor Roosevelt
invited her to sing on the steps of the Lincoln Memorial. 75,000 people
came to hear her.

In 1955 Marian became the first African American to sing a leading
part at the Metropolitan Opera in New York City. She retired in 1965,
after many recordings. She died in 1993, at the age of 96.

TIMELINE

Marian Anderson		America
was born on February 17	**1897**	
	1918	**A. Philip Randolph** was arrested for making an anti-war speech
	1919	Black singer, actor, scholar, athlete Paul Robeson graduated from Rutgers University
won a singing contest	**1923**	**Duke Kahanamoku** won a silver medal at the Paris Olympics
gave a recital in New York City began a world tour	**1924**	
	1932	**Franklin D. Roosevelt** was elected President
sang on the steps of the Lincoln Memorial	**1939**	
became the first African American to sing at the Metropolitan Opera	**1955**	the Montgomery, Alabama, bus boycott began
	1960	**John Kennedy** was elected President
	1963	the March on Washington ended up at the Lincoln Memorial
retired from singing	**1965**	
	1968	**Martin Luther King, Jr.** was assassinated
died at the age of 96	**1993**	**Cesar Chavez** died at 66

Research:

www.afrovoices.com/anderson.html

Katharine Hepburn

1907–2003

Katharine Hepburn was born in Hartford, Connecticut, in 1907. As a child, she liked to put on plays with the other children in her neighborhood. After college, she began to act in stage plays. By 1928 she was a well-known actress on Broadway.

Katharine began her film career in 1932. The next year, she appeared in a movie called *Morning Glory*. She won an Academy Award for her performance in that film. She was also named Best Actress for her roles in *Guess Who's Coming to Dinner?* (1967), *The Lion in Winter* (1968), and *On Golden Pond* (1981). Critics and fans have also praised her performance in *The African Queen* (1952).

People admired Katharine Hepburn for her strength and independence. In her own words, she was "tall, skinny, and very determined." In her later years, she continued to work even though she had arthritis and Parkinson's disease. Katharine Hepburn died in 2003 at the age of 96.

TIMELINE

Katharine Hepburn		America
was born in Hartford, Connecticut, November 8	**1907**	
	1908	Henry Ford introduced the Model T car
	1923	the first motion picture with sound was shown
became a well-known actress on Broadway in New York City	**1928**	
began her film career	**1932**	**FDR** was elected President
received her 1st Oscar (an Academy Award) for *Morning Glory*	**1933**	
	1939	the movie, *The Wizard of Oz,* based on **L. Frank Baum's** children's book, was released
starred in *The African Queen* with Humphrey Bogart	**1952**	
	1956	*My Fair Lady* opened on Broadway
	1958	**Alvin Ailey** founded his Dance Theater
won best actress Oscar for *Guess Who's Coming to Dinner*	**1967**	
won 3rd Oscar for *The Lion in Winter*	**1968**	
won 4th Oscar for *On Golden Pond*	**1981**	Actor Ronald Reagan became President at the age of 69
died at the age of 96	**2003**	
	2004	Reagan died at 92

Research:
www.katharinehepburn.net/

Harry Houdini

1874 –1926

Harry Houdini was born in Hungary in 1874. His family moved to America in 1875. As a young boy, Harry started doing magic tricks to make money. In 1893 he performed at the World's Fair in Chicago. People were amused by his tricks, and Harry decided to take his show on the road.

Harry toured the country, and in 1900 he went on a tour of Europe. In each show, he was handcuffed, tied up with rope, and locked in a trunk. The trunk was then covered with a curtain. Within a minute, Harry had untied the rope and freed himself from the handcuffs. When he came out from behind the curtain, people were astonished and amazed.

Harry returned to America in 1905 with new tricks for his fans. Sometimes he was sealed in a large milk can full of water, for example, but he always managed to escape. In 1919 he created an illusion called the "Vanishing Elephant Trick." Again, the audience was thrilled and mystified.

Harry was injured during a show on October 24, 1926. He died a week later, on Halloween night. His funeral was held in New York City and was attended by thousands of people.

TIMELINE

Harry Houdini		America
was born in Hungary	**1874**	
family moved to America	**1875**	
	1878	**Edison** invented the electric light
	1985	**Annie Oakley** and **Sitting Bull** joined Buffalo Bill's Wild West Show
	1886	The Statue of Liberty opened
	1987	Buffalo Bill toured England
	1888	the Kodak box camera was introduced
	1892	Ellis Island was opened
performed at the World's Fair	**1893**	
went on a tour of Europe	**1900**	
	1901	President McKinley was assassinated Vice-President Theodore Roosevelt became President
returned to America	**1905**	
	1906	San Francisco was hit by an earthquake
created the "Vanishing Elephant" trick	**1919**	
	1921	Congress set immigration quotas
injured during a show died on Halloween night	**1926**	Irish immigrant **Father Flanagan** named his home "Boys Town"

Research:

www.magictricks.com/houdini/bio.htm

Alvin Ailey

1931 −1989

Alvin Ailey was born in a small town in Texas in 1931, but he grew up in Los Angeles, California. In 1945 Alvin's class went on a field trip to see a Russian dance troupe. It was the first time Alvin had ever seen a dance concert, and he was fascinated by it. Later, he saw a performance by a famous African American dance troupe, an experience that changed his life. For the first time, Alvin thought he might make a living as a dancer.

Alvin enrolled in a dance school in 1948, and he studied with some of the best teachers of the time. He began to choreograph his own dances, and in 1954 he moved to New York City. In 1958 he presented his first production, and the Alvin Ailey Dance Theater was born. Alvin produced many other dance concerts in the coming years. One of his best-known works is *Revelations*, which was first performed in 1960. Like many of Alvin's other productions, it combined gospel music, black spirituals, and small-town religion.

Alvin stopped dancing in 1965 so he could concentrate on choreography. His shows were high-energy, flashy, and had elaborate set designs. Many people who had never liked ballet came to see Alvin's productions. He introduced a whole generation of people to modern ballet.

Alvin Ailey died of AIDS in 1989. In his lifetime, he had created over 79 ballets. Since his death, the Alvin Ailey Dance Theater has continued to thrill audiences around the world.

TIMELINE

Alvin Ailey		America
was born in Texas	**1931**	
	1941	the U.S. joined World War II
saw a Russian dance troup	**1945**	World War II ended
enrolled in dance school	**1948**	Jackie Robinson broke baseball's color barrier
began to do his own ballet choreography	**1954**	*Brown vs Board of Education* banned segregation in public schools
founded the Alvin Ailey Dance Theater	**1958**	
Revelations appeared for the first time	**1960**	overcoming childhood polio, **Wilma Rudolph** won three gold medals at the Rome Olympics
stopped dancing to concentrate on choreography	**1964**	**Martin Luther King, Jr.** was given the Nobel Peace Prize
	1965	Malcolm X was assassinated
	1967	**Katharine Hepburn** won an Oscar for *Guess Who's Coming to Dinner*
	1981	AIDS was recognized as an epidemic
died of AIDS	**1989**	

Research:
www.texas-on-line.com/graphic/alvinailey.htm

Roberto Clemente

1934–1972

Roberto Clemente was born in Puerto Rico in 1934. He loved to play baseball. But his family didn't have very much money. Roberto had to make his own baseball equipment. Roberto joined a baseball team in high school. He started to play professional baseball in 1951 for the Montreal Royals.

He began playing in the American Major Leagues with the Pittsburgh Pirates in 1955. Clemente helped the Pirates win the World Series in 1960. And in 1966, he was voted the Most Valuable Player. He played for the Pirates for 18 years. He is in the National Baseball Hall of Fame.

Clemente died in a plane crash in 1972. He was flying supplies to the victims of an earthquake in Nicaragua.

TIMELINE

Roberto Clemente		America
was born in Puerto Rico	**1934**	
	1936	the Baseball Hall of Fame was established in Cooperstown, NY.
	1948	Jackie Robinson became the first black player in the Major Leagues
joined the Montreal Royals	**1951**	the first transcontinental TV started
	1952	Puerto Rico became a commonwealth
began to play for the Pittsburgh Pirates	**1955**	**Dr. King** organized the Montgomery bus boycott started by Rosa Parks
helped the Pirates win the World Series	**1960**	**JFK** was elected President
was voted the Most Valuable Player	**1966**	athlete **Bruce Lee's** acting career began on *The Green Hornet* TV series
died in a plane crash	**1972**	an earthquake hit Nicaragua
was elected to the National Baseball Hall of Fame	**1973**	

Research:

www.robertoclemente21.com/Biography/biography.html

Wilma Rudolph

1940 – 1994

Wilma Rudolph was born in 1940 in Tennessee. At the time, there was a polio epidemic in Tennessee. Wilma caught the disease when she was five years old. She got a high fever that lasted for a long time. When the fever was over, she could barely walk. Wilma had to wear a leg brace to walk. Her mother massaged her legs, and Wilma practiced walking every day.

Wilma put away her leg brace when she turned 11. She could finally walk, all by herself. Wilma loved to walk and run. In high school, she joined a track team. She was so good that she was in the Olympic Games in 1956. She ran a relay race, and won a bronze medal.

But Wilma's greatest achievement came at the next Olympic Games, in 1960. That year, Wilma won three gold medals. In 1984 she was named one of America's five "Greatest Women Athletes."

TIMELINE

Wilma Rudolph		America
was born in Tennessee, June 23	**1940**	
became sick with polio	**1945**	polio survivor, **President Franklin Roosevelt** died
was finally able to walk without a leg brace	**1951**	
	1955	Dr. Salk's polio vaccine became available
won a bronze medal for running a relay race at the Olympics	**1956**	the Olympic Games were held in Australia
won three gold medals at Rome insisted her homecoming "victory parade" back in Clarksville, Tennessee, be desegregated	**1960**	The Olympics were held in Rome **John Kennedy** was elected President
	1967	Muhammad Ali refused military service during the Vietnam War
	1972	**Roberto Clemente** was killed in a plane crash
	1975	Arthur Ashe retired from tennis
named one of America's five "Greatest Women Athletes"	**1984**	
died in Nashville at 54	**1994**	

Research:

www.espn.go.com/sportscentury/features/00016444.html

Bruce Lee

1940–1973

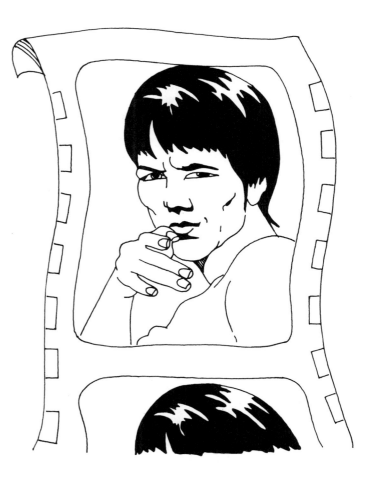

Bruce Lee was born in 1940. He and his family lived in Chinatown, a neighborhood in San Francisco, California. Bruce was sickly and weak as a child. He decided to learn martial arts to protect himself. He exercised and practiced his moves constantly. Eventually, he opened his own martial arts studio. In the early 1960s, he developed his own style of kung fu, called jeet kune do.

Bruce became well known. He even started to give private lessons to movie stars. In 1966 he appeared in a TV series called *The Green Hornet*. Bruce wanted to do more films. But most movie directors didn't want to take a chance on a Chinese actor. So Bruce decided to move to Hong Kong.

Bruce's career took off in Hong Kong. In 1971 he starred in two films called *The Big Boss* and *Fist of Fury*. They were smash hits. Bruce decided to make his own films after that. He was a producer, director, writer, and actor.

In 1973 Bruce was making a movie called *Enter the Dragon*. He died during the production, under mysterious circumstances. *Enter the Dragon* was released after his death, and it has become one of Bruce's most popular films.

TIMELINE

Bruce Lee		America
was born in San Francisco	**1940**	**Wilma Rudolph** was born
	1941	Pearl Harbor was bombed U.S. entered World War II
	1950	the Korean War began
	1952	**Katharine Hepburn** starred in *The African Queen*
	1957	*The Bridge Over the River Kwai* won the Academy Award for best picture
opened his own studio developed his own style of kung fu	**1960s**	
starred in *The Green Hornet*	**1966**	the U.S. bombed Hanoi
	1969	the Woodstock Music Festival was held
moved to Hong Kong made two films	**1971**	
	1972	**Roberto Clemente** was killed in an airplane crash
died while making *Enter the Dragon*	**1973**	

Research:
www.allbrucelee.com

Duke Kahanamoku

1890–1968

Duke Paoa Kahanamoku was born in Hawaii. He was a full-blooded Hawaiian who grew up near the ocean and loved to swim. As he got older, Duke learned to surf. In his teens, Duke dropped out of high school and joined a surf club. He became the group's leader and set a good example for healthy living. He didn't drink or smoke, and he avoided getting into fights.

In 1911 Duke entered a swimming contest. He beat all the other swimmers and broke two world records. After several other competitions, he qualified for the Olympics. In 1912 he won a gold medal, breaking the record for the 100-meter freestyle.

After the Olympics, Duke traveled throughout the world to participate in exhibitions and swimming meets. In 1912 he helped surfing become popular in southern California, and in 1915 he did the same in Australia.

The Olympics were not held in 1916 because of World War I, but Duke trained Red Cross workers in lifesaving and helped the Red Cross raise money.

Duke broke his own record and won the gold again in the 1920 Olympics, but in 1924, at the age of 34, he was defeated by Johnny Weissmuller, and he won "only" the silver medal. Later, Duke explained that he had lost to Tarzan. (Weissmuller went on to be Tarzan in the movies.)

Duke Kahanamoku died of a heart attack in 1968, while he was on the beach in Waikiki, his hometown. His ashes were scattered over the Pacific Ocean. He is known today as the "father of modern surfing."

TIMELINE

Duke Kahanamoku		America
was born in Hawaii	**1890**	
	1898	the U.S. annexed Hawaii
	1899	**Princess Kaiulani** died
entered a swimming contest broke two world records	**1911**	
won a gold medal at the Olympics	**1912**	the Olympics were held in Stockholm, Sweden
raised money for the Red Cross	**1914**	World War I started in Europe it ended at 11 a.m. on 11/11/1918
won a second Olympic gold medal	**1920**	Antwerp, Belgium, hosted the Olympics
won an Olympic silver medal was beaten by Johnny Weissmuller	**1924**	the Olympics were held in Paris, France
made the first of ten movies in which he had minor roles	**1925**	
	1937	**Amelia Earhart** disappeared while flying across the Pacific
	1941	Pearl Harbor (HI) was bombed
	1949	Hawaii became a state
played a native chief in the Oscar- winning film *Mr. Roberts*	**1955**	**Roberto Clemente** began playing for the Pittsburgh Pirates
died of a heart attack on the beach in Waikiki	**1968**	

Research:

www.hawaiiweb.com/html/duke_kahanamoku_statue.html

Comparative Timeline 1730–1890

	1730	1740	1750	1760	1770	1780	1790	1800	1810	1820	1830	1840	1850	1860	1870	1880	1890

George Washington •1732 — 1799•

Daniel Boone •1734 — 1820•

John Paul Jones •1747 — 1792•

Sequoyah •1770 — 1842•

Johnny Appleseed •1774 — 1845•

Sacagawea •1786 — 1812•

Sojourner Truth •1797 — 1883•

Robert E. Lee •1807 — 1870•

Abraham Lincoln •1809 — 1865•

Frederick Douglass •1817 — 1895•

Susan B. Anthony •1820 — > (1906)

Clara Barton •1821 — > (1912)

Harriet Tubman •1821 — > (1913)

105

Comparative Timeline 1820-1970

1820 1830 1840 1850 1860 1870 1880 1890 1900 1910 1920 1930 1940 1950 1960 1970

Emily Dickinson •1830 — 1886•

Mother Jones •1830 — 1930•

Sitting Bull •1834 — 1890•

Mark Twain •1835 — 1910•

Andrew Carnegie •1835 — 1919•

Chief Joseph •1840 — 1904•

Sarah Winnemucca •1844 — 1891•

Thomas Edison •1847 — 1931•

Nat Love •1854 — 1921•

Booker T. Washington •1856 — 1915•

L. Frank Baum •1856 — 1919•

Annie Oakley •1860 — 1926•

Jane Addams •1860 — 1935•

106

Comparative Timeline 1850-2000

| 1850 | 1860 | 1870 | 1880 | 1890 | 1900 | 1910 | 1920 | 1930 | 1940 | 1950 | 1960 | 1970 | 1980 | 1990 | 2000 |

•1861 George Washington Carver 1943•

•1864 Nellie Bly 1922•

•1866 Matthew Henson 1955•

•1874 Harry Houdini 1926•

•1875 1899• Princess Kaiulani

•1882 Franklin D. Roosevelt 1945•

•1886 Father Flanagan 1948•

•1889 A. Philip Randolph 1979•

•1890 Duke Kahanamoku 1968•

•1891 Zora Neale Hurston 1960•

•1897 1937• Amelia Earhart

•1897 Marian Anderson 1993•

•1907 Rachel Carson 1964•

Comparative Timeline 1900–2020

1900	1910	1920	1930	1940	1950	1960	1970	1980	1990	2000	2010	2020

•1907   Katharine Hepburn   2003•

•1910   Jacqueline Cochran   1980•

•1910   Annie Dodge Wauneka   1997•

•1917   John F. Kennedy   1963•

•1921   William Kenzo Nakamura   1944•

•1923   Alan Shepard   1998•

•1927   Cesar Chavez   1993•

•1929   Martin Luther King, Jr.   1968•

•1931   Alvin Ailey   1989•

•1932   Dian Fossey   1985•

•1934   Roberto Clemente   1972•

•1940   Wilma Rudolph   1994•

•1940   Bruce Lee   1973•

List of U.S. Presidents and Events

1789	George Washington	first President; government established
1797	John Adams	capital moved to Washington, D.C.
1801	Thomas Jefferson	Louisiana Purchase
1809	James Madison	War of 1812
1817	James Monroe	slavery abolished in Illinois
1825	John Quincy Adams	Erie Canal opened
1829	Andrew Jackson	Texas independence
1837	Martin Van Buren	the "Trail of Tears"
1841	William Henry Harrison (D)	*(died after one month in office)*
1841	John Tyler	pioneers move west
1845	James Polk	war with Mexico
1849	Zachary Taylor (D)	California Gold Rush
1850	Millard Fillmore	California statehood
1853	Franklin Pierce	Republican Party formed
1857	James Buchanan	oil discovered in Pennsylvania
1861	Abraham Lincoln (A)	Civil War
1865	Andrew Johnson	Alaska purchased
1869	Ulysses S. Grant	Chicago fire
1877	Rutherford B. Hayes	first telephone exchange
1881	James A. Garfield (A)	Red Cross founded
1881	Chester A. Arthur	Brooklyn Bridge opened
1885	Grover Cleveland	American Federation of Labor
1889	Benjamin Harrison	Ellis Island opened
1893	Grover Cleveland	financial panic; Pullman strike
1897	William McKinley (A)	Spanish-American War
1901	Theodore Roosevelt	oil in Texas; Model T car
1909	William Howard Taft	first transcontinental flight
1913	Woodrow Wilson	World War I; Panama Canal
1921	Warren G. Harding (D)	immigration quotas set; scandal
1923	Calvin Coolidge	Lindbergh flew the Atlantic solo
1929	Herbert Hoover	stock market crash; Depression begins
1933	Franklin D. Roosevelt (D)	the New Deal; World War II
1945	Harry S. Truman	Atom Bomb; Korean War
1953	Dwight D. Eisenhower	Montgomery bus boycott
1961	John F. Kennedy (A)	Cuban Missile Crisis
1963	Lyndon B. Johnson	Vietnam War
1969	Richard M. Nixon (R)	Watergate
1974	Gerald R. Ford	Saigon fell
1977	Jimmy Carter	Embassy in Iran crisis
1981	Ronald Reagan	hostages freed in Iran; Cold War ended
1989	George H. W. Bush	Gulf War
1993	Bill Clinton	relations with Vietnam resumed
2001	George W. Bush	9/11; invasion of Iraq

D = died in office   A = assassinated   R = resigned

Other Publications on American history and culture

American Holidays

Exploring Traditions, Customs, and Backgrounds

This is a cultural reader. The 4th of July, Election Day, Christmas, Martin Luther King's Birthday, and New Year's Eve: reading about our American national holidays is not only fun, it is a way of exploring our diverse culture and values. How do we celebrate Memorial Day? What is the history of Thanksgiving? What does "Be my valentine" mean? And then there are other holidays special to specific cultural and religious groups: Chinese New Year, Kwanzaa, and Cinco de Mayo and the major Christian, Muslim, and Jewish religious holidays. The appendix includes historical readings, traditonal holiday songs, state holidays, and gift-giving customs.

But this is more than a cultural reader; it's also **a vocabulary development text** that both focuses on specific words (in bold in the text) and teaches vocabulary acquisition skills. Students match the key words to definitions and do exercises introducing them to the noun, verb, adverb, and adjective forms of the words.

A **CD** for building listening skills is available.

Plays for the Holidays

Historical and Cultural Celebrations.
13 brief plays from Labor Day (Peter MaGuire organizes immigrant workers) to Independence Day (Writing the Declaration of Independence in Philadelphia). The *dramatis personae* include Columbus, The Headless Horseman, Eisenhower, Scrooge, Pocahontas, Rosa Parks, JFK, Washington, Franklin, and more.

All Around America

The Time Traveler's Talk Show.
The show stops at 18 famous places around the U.S. Students read the script, which includes a host, a local guide, guests from the past, and callers from the present. Supplemented with an **Activities Workbook** that builds language skills, with emphasis on idiomatic spoken language. All the scripts are also recorded on two **CDs** for listening practice.

Celebrating American Heroes

The Playbook is a collection of 13 short plays featuring an interesting group of heroes, from the very famous (Lincoln, Washington, Edison) to the less well-known (Dolley Madison, Jonas Salk, John Muir, Cesar Chavez, Harriet Beecher Stowe). The format of the plays is similar to *Plays for the Holidays,* with a few leading characters, a narrator, and a chorus. **The photocopyable Teacher's Guide** includes several pronunciation and vocabulary worksheets. A dramatic recording of the plays is also available on cassette or CD.

Heroes from American History

An integrated skills, content-based reader for intermediate ESL. All the heroes in the playbook (above) are featured, as well as Maya Lin, Eleanor Roosevelt, and the "ordinary citizen." There are maps and timelines that bring out the historical context of the times when these heroes lived.

Living in the United States

A brief introduction to U.S. culture
Part One: Basic Survival Information.
Part Two: Customs and Values.
Part Three: Country Facts.

North American Indian Tales

48 animal stories collected from tribes across North America. The tales explain how the world came to be as it is *(How Chipmunk Got Her Stripes,* etc.) Each story is on a separate card with a colorful illustration by a popular Native American artist.

For information or to order, visit our webstore
www.ProLinguaAssociates.com *or call our*
Inquiries/Advice Hotline (800) 366-4775.
Email: Info@ProLinguaAssociates.com